Camino Chronicle

WALKING TO SANTIAGO

Camino Chronicle

WALKING TO SANTIAGO

Susan Alcorn

Shepherd Canyon Books
Oakland, California

To my dear friend Angie
Buen camino! Love!
Susan Alcorn

Shepherd Canyon Books
Oakland, CA 94611, U.S.A.
(866) 219-8260 or (510) 339-3441
www.backpack45.com

ISBN-13: 978-0-936034-03-4
ISBN-10: 0-936034-03-3

Library of Congress Control Number 2006900597

Publisher's Cataloging-in-Publication Data

Alcorn, Susan.
   Camino chronicle : walking to Santiago / Susan Alcorn.
   p. cm.
   Includes bibliographical references and index.
   ISBN 0-936034-03-3
   ISBN 13 978-0-936034-03-4
1. Christian pilgrims and pilgrimages--Spain--Santiago de Compostela. 2. Hiking--Spain--Guidebooks. 3. Backpacking--Spain--Guidebooks. 4. Spain--Description and travel. I. Title.

GV199.44.S7 A43 2006
796.52/209--dc22   2006900597

To Haley, Madison, and Logan with love

"The world is a book, and those who do not travel, read only a page."

—Saint Augustine of Hippo

Contents

*Readers who compare various guidebooks to the Camino de Santiago will notice that different authors use different criteria for defining the various regions encountered on the Camino. We have used the five geographic divisions suggested by the Confraternity of Saint James in their *Pilgrim Guides to Spain, 1. The Camino Francés.* These regions are: the Pyrenees, West Navarra/La Rioja, the Meseta, the mountains of the Cantabrian, and Galicia. The mileages/kilometers given in this book have been rounded to the nearest five-tenths. The Confraternity's annually updated book will be referred to as the *Pilgrim Guide* in this book.

THIS IS A true story as experienced by the author. Some names have been changed to maintain the privacy of those individuals.

Legends and Essays

Preface

Serendipity: "The faculty or phenomenon of finding valuable or agreeable things not sought for."
—Merriam-Webster's *Collegiate Dictionary*, 10th edition

Serendipity, how else can it be explained? In June 2001, less than three months before Ralph and I were to start our Camino hike, we found ourselves at a dinner party for our close friends Carol and Jim. We felt honored to be included in the small group of friends who had been invited to help celebrate their anniversary. We were gathered at the same small hotel where they had held their garden wedding five years earlier.

Because Jim had formerly been a priest and Carol had attended theological school, the guest list was not an unusual one for them. But for us, it was an unusual social setting: a priest, a former priest, various "lay leaders." The spiritual world we best relate to is less formal; we love the out-of-doors. So when we were seated at the long, white cloth-covered table and I found myself across from Father Paul, I began searching for some common topic for discussion.

To my delight, Father Paul turned out to be a very entertaining companion. He obviously enjoyed his wine at least as much as the rest of us. He was a great storyteller, and he didn't even once quote parables from the Bible. Father Paul raised his glass to toast Jim and Carol's anniversary, and we were soon all talking, laughing, and enjoying our dinner. But there was a bittersweet taste to the occasion. One of the guests, Andrew, had just had cancer surgery. We hoped all was well and that he was now cancer-free, but no one could predict that with any certainty. Andrew announced that he was going to move; he was only hours away from leaving the San Francisco Bay Area and entering a monastery. He was leaving his apartment and giving away the last of his possessions: the ones he had held onto until the end, the ones hardest to part with.

"I have something for each of you," he stated. "I just have to go out to my car and get them." Soon, he was back carrying an armload of books. "These are some of my favorite books; please take whichever you want."

The title of one jumped out at me: a book about the Camino de Santiago, Paulo Coelho's *The Pilgrimage*, which just that afternoon had been mentioned by someone in my monthly writers' group. I'd automatically put it on a mental list to look for and here it was, sitting before me. I hesitated. I didn't want to take what someone else wanted. I had just met Andrew; others were close friends. Seconds passed. No one reached out. Then I did. I knew it was meant to be.

Our first notice of the Camino was in the mid-1990s. Ralph happened upon an article in the travel section of our newspaper, the *San Francisco Chronicle*. Like many other travel articles we'd found, it got filed. It was of interest, but we didn't have any immediate plans for such an extensive trip. And it wasn't on my "life list" of trips that Ralph and I would occasionally talk about taking some day. My list included such things as visiting the game parks of Africa, trekking in Nepal, and returning to Alaska to see the grizzly bears.

But in the intervening years, we'd started to consider the benefits of early retirement. I wanted more personal time so that I could finish writing, and publish, my previous book, *We're in the Mountains Not Over the Hill—Tales and Tips from Seasoned Women Backpackers*. We wanted to finish hiking California's John Muir Trail. And, finally, we envisioned the opportunity to take off for the six weeks we'd need to go to Spain and hike the Camino.

Now it had happened, at least in part: I had retired, and Ralph had a more flexible work schedule. And so, at Jim and Carol's celebration, we were also celebrating my recent retirement.

Even though our plans for hiking the Camino were well underway (I had already made the reservations for our flights and our initial stay in Madrid, and Ralph had been pouring over the guidebooks), I was nervous about the prospect of hiking the 500 miles across northern Spain. *The Pilgrimage* practically dropping into my lap at the dinner helped; I needed all the encouragement I could get.

In August of that same year, we backpacked 60 miles of the John Muir Trail, thereby completing the 211-mile route that travels through the highest mountain passes of the Sierra Nevada. Having just accomplished that last segment, which included going over a couple of passes topping 10,000 feet, I felt fit and confident to tackle anything Spain's portion of the Pyrenees could offer.

Then, only days before our scheduled September departure, my back began to go into painful spasms (which seemed to occur about twice a year). Ralph and I talked about options. I recalled advice I had received earlier about backpacking trips: always know where the nearest trailhead is. Ralph could hike alone if need be; I could hop on a bus if necessary.

IT WAS DURING that time of uncertainty that I wrote the first entry in my journal about the Camino trip:

AUGUST 20, 2001

WE'RE PLANNING TO walk across Spain on the Camino de Santiago, the famous pilgrimage trail. It's scary as hell. I'm worried that my body (my feet, my knees, or my back) will fail me. My spirit will be weak, I'll be irritable, and cry. I'm convinced I'll be hot and miserable, which should be okay, in and of itself, but that I'll be a wimp about it doesn't feel okay. I wonder why it's so important to me to succeed at this trip. How can I learn to enjoy the journey, to celebrate each day the accomplishment of hiking several miles, and to let go of being so goal-oriented that I feel satisfied only when I have the 500 miles behind me?

The reality is that even experienced hikers and travelers may go into this adventure with not only excitement and anticipation, but also some concerns. That's understandable, particularly when you consider that a long-distance hike of this sort is not something that most of us have much, if any, experience with.

AS YOU'LL SOON discover, however, it's an achievable, rewarding goal. And those who undertake the journey learn to deal with the physical demands and logistical details on a day-to-day basis. In my case, the back pain subsided, my usual optimism returned, and we set out for our pilgrimage through Spain.

Once on the trip, I realized I didn't know nearly as much about the Camino as it warranted; our pre-trip reading had only scratched the surface as far as understanding all that we were seeing and experiencing. When we returned home, I decided to delve deeper into the traditions and history of Spain and its Camino.

Now I'm pleased to pass on to you the legends and stories, combined with my personal observations and experiences as recorded in my journal, that will provide you with a greater understanding of why millions have been drawn to the Camino de Santiago and the city of Santiago de Compostela.

IF YOU EMBARK on this trip, it will require courage, determination, and resiliency, but you will be amply rewarded with a sense of accomplishment, with a deeper knowledge and understanding of Spain's culture and history, and with countless opportunities to "be in the moment." You'll undoubtedly experience great beauty and joy.

It is my sincere hope that this book will provide those who want to make the pilgrimage to Santiago de Compostela with the combination of history and trail wisdom that will guarantee a rich and meaningful trip.

Buen Camino!

Susan Alcorn

Acknowledgements

Rarely are books written without the help of many people; this work is no exception. First, I want to thank my husband, Ralph, whose love and support keep me afloat even through the dark moments. In addition, he's my partner on the trail and in the publishing business.

I am very appreciative of the valuable editing help and encouraging support given by the non-fiction group of the California Writers' Club, Berkeley Chapter. Thank you Virginia Anderson (chairperson until her death in 2005), Charles Loughran, Marlin Griffin, Mary Ann Brewin, Otto and Phyllis Smith, Cynthia Tilden, and Judith Gussman.

Thanks to Denise Roessle, a close friend whom I greatly admire for her dedication to the craft of writing and to the importance of authentic writing. I find her to be both an inspiration and a source of continuing support.

Thank you to Donna Miller for reading the manuscript and providing helpful feedback. Donna was my "job-share" teaching partner for third graders in Hercules, California. Donna's willingness to accommodate my travel schedule while I was in Spain, and her supportive manner with our students and me, has made her a dear friend.

Thanks also to Joan Olson, another teacher and friend, for editing suggestions. Joan has always encouraged me, my writing, and my travels, and was a delightful e-mail correspondent while I was hiking the Camino.

Thanks to Fran Alcorn for reading and commenting on the manuscript, thereby demonstrating her interest in my adventures and her interest in history.

I want to express my gratitude and appreciation to Melanie Rigney, "Editor for You," for her tactful and well-reasoned evaluation of my manuscript and her clear suggestions for improvements.

Likewise, thanks to Kathy Morey, author of several books published by Wilderness Press, who helped edit and fine-tune this book. Her professionalism and encouragement is much appreciated.

I found Kathy Gower, Rosina Lila, and Eldor Pederson to be quite helpful. All are active contributors to the Camino forums. Eldor clarified the use of "hospital, hospice, and *Hospitales*" as commonly used in documents about medieval pilgrimage.

Thank you to Eileen Gardiner, Ph.D., of Italica Press, Inc.; Esther Robinson of St. Martin's Press; Shelley Keller, writer, and Georgette Jeppesen, editor, of *Solano Magazine*; Dorothy Strakele of *Costco Connection*; and Matt Zaleski from andre-norton.org for giving permission to reprint from various sources.

I GREATLY VALUE the correspondence I had with many of our friends and family while we were on the Camino. Their reports on happenings at home were especially helpful following the events of 9/11. I used only a small percentage of the messages sent to us. The following e-mail correspondents are included:

Marcy del Clements, whose great backpacking stories led me to interview and include her in my previous book. Marcy's now in her sixties, yet it appears that her backpacking trips have become more challenging and adventurous with each passing year.

Melanie Clark and her husband, Bob Miller, who are long-time friends that I can always count on to keep me up to date on political happenings and world events.

Lynn Coulter, who is a member of our family. Lynn nowadays handles our fulfillment orders for our publishing company in our absence.

Lorinda Ferland and her husband, Bob Doerr, who are close friends with whom we have shared dozens of holidays and dinner parties (often ending with the offering of custard pie).

Karen and Mike Herzog, family members who, after spending a couple of intense years pursuing an overseas adoption, and after 9/11, a couple of frantic days, managed to bring their beautiful adopted baby, Sarah, home from Russia. All are now happily settled in the S. F. Bay Area.

Sue Ann Jones, Pat Asvitt, and Jean Morris, who have been my friends for almost fifty years, dating back to high school when we were all living in Richmond, California.

Doris Klein, who I met when I was interviewing backpackers for my earlier book. I am in awe of Doris because of her years of public service and her long list of trails hiked. She has led local groups hiking, and her Jane Muir Trail group backpacking, for well over a quarter century.

Sandy Simmons, with whom I taught for several years and to whose excellence as a teacher I always aspired. She generously shared her heartfelt concerns about 9/11: the future of our country and the safety of her sons who were in the service. She and her husband, Craig, have become our "trail angels" by driving us to trailheads for our continuing backpacking trips on the Pacific Crest Trail.

Janet Valentine, our friend and neighbor, who watched our house and challenging cats while we were in Spain.

Other friends and family who deserve my thanks: Joyce Alcorn, Joyce and Brian Bender, Scott and Tom Cole, Tracy Chupp and Mike Prym, and Rose Offner.

Introduction to the Camino de Santiago
A Brief History for Contemporary Travelers

We are not in a position in which we have nothing to work with.
We already have capacities, talents, direction, missions, callings.
—Abraham Maslow, psychologist

The Camino de Santiago, also called the *Camino Francés* or *The French Way*, is a 500-mile route across northern Spain, starting in the Pyrenees on the French border and ending at Santiago de Compostela in Galicia in the northwest of Spain. This pilgrimage route, which can be followed on foot, bike, or by horseback, is more than a thousand years old. Traditionally, the pilgrimage was made to reach the cathedral in Santiago de Compostela to visit the remains of St. James, the disciple.

Santiago (meaning *Saint James the Greater* or *Elder* in English and *Saint Jacque* in French) was one of Jesus's twelve original apostles. His brother John was also an apostle; both were the sons of Zebedee and Salome and were fishermen on the Sea of Galilee until Jesus asked them to join his ministry.

1

After the crucifixion of Jesus, James set out for Spain. Some accounts state that James was not particularly successful in converting the locals to Christianity (only seven) and he returned to Jerusalem. There, in 44 CE, Herod Agrippa I beheaded him.

The legend continues: friends took the body to the sea and placed it in a stone boat with no oars, sails, or crew and pushed the boat offshore. The boat was carried by the winds and angels through the Pillars of Hercules (the two promontories at the eastern end of the Strait of Gibraltar) to Spain. There it came ashore at Padron on the Galician coast: twenty kilometers from what is now the city of Santiago de Compostela. His remains were brought by two of his disciples a short distance inland and buried. His tomb was soon forgotten.

Over the next several centuries, Christianity became more widespread throughout Spain. In the 700s, Muslim (Moorish) armies came from North Africa and rapidly conquered much of Spain and continued toward France. Nevertheless, pockets of Christianity remained, particularly in northwestern Spain.

Around 813, music and twinkling stars drew a Christian hermit, Pelayo, to the remote hillside where St. James's remains had been long interred. He found bones at the site. A local bishop declared that the bones were those of St. James and his two disciples. Soon after, Alfonso II, King of Asturias, visited the site and had a small chapel built there. He proclaimed St. James to be the Patron Saint of Spain.

Visitors began to come to view the tomb and chapel; gradually a town began to develop around the hillside. (The name *Compostela* of the "de Compostela" is, according to some sources, from the original name Alfonso gave the site: Campus de la Stella [*campus stellae (L.)*] or "field of the stars." Santiago de Compostela translates to "St. James of the star field.")

In the mid-800s Muslims still controlled most of the Iberian peninsula, but Christianity was not dead. Visions of St. James increased; many claimed they saw him battle the Muslims. The most famous sighting was in 852. There, at the Battle of Clavijo (near Logroño), he appeared as a warrior, mounted on a charging white horse, to lead the Christians to a victorious defeat of their Muslim enemies. Tens of thousands of Moors were killed in the decisive battle and St. James acquired still another name, *Santiago Matamoros* (Moor-slayer).

The number of pilgrims making their way to the tomb of St. James continued to grow. Over time, the original chapel was replaced by increasingly larger ones. Travelers, needing food and shelter for their long journey, brought commerce and prosperity to the towns and monasteries that grew along the route. *Hospitales* (precursors to the present day refuges/refugios) provided a place to spend the night and obtain food. They also provided medical assistance to those who needed it. Most villages along the route catered to the pilgrims; some preyed upon them.

MAKING A PILGRIMAGE may be difficult for people today to imagine, but in medieval times it was much in the public's consciousness. Though holy places abounded in Europe, for Christians there were three major holy cities: Santiago de Compostela, Rome, and Jerusalem. "Palm bringers" came to mean those who traveled to Jerusalem, "Rome-goers" those who visited that city, and "pilgrimage" became identified with the journey to Santiago.

In earlier pilgrimage times, people embarked on the journey for various reasons, but principally for religious ones: the forgiveness of sins or to proclaim their faith. Reaching Santiago was the goal, but for some who died en route, the *attempt* was enough to guarantee forgiveness. Some were forced to go as an alternative to prison (much as the army was an alternative given to youthful troublemakers here in the 1950s). And some speculate that others went as tourists to add excitement to their medieval lives.

TRADITIONALLY, PEOPLE WOULD set out from their own doorsteps to make their pilgrimage to Santiago; it was a journey that would take them several months or more to complete. Today's travelers can choose among dozens of the original pilgrim routes from throughout Europe (four from France alone) that lead to the Camino.

In general Europeans are more aware of the numerous routes because they are "in their own backyard" so to speak, but Americans of European descent, if they were to collect the stories of their ancestors from just a few generations back, would undoubtedly find some who had followed this ancient network of trails. When my husband Ralph and I set out to hike the trail, we learned from one of his aunts, who is of Norwegian descent, that someone in each generation of her family (until the current one) had made the pilgrimage from Norway to Santiago on horseback. South Americans (Brazilians in particular) are aware of the Camino because of their strong ties to the Catholic Church.

For the pilgrim of medieval times, packing was not difficult. The garb consisted chiefly of a coarsely woven tunic covered with a long, heavy wool cloak for protection from the weather and to serve as a blanket for the traveler at nightfall when he slept by trail's edge. The tunic was fastened with a belt; a pouch hung from his belt for food. His wide-brimmed hat was decorated with scallop shells. He carried a heavy staff for walking and for fighting off wolves and bandits. And from the staff hung a hollowed out gourd for carrying water. A pair of thick, leather sandals completed the outfit.

Nowadays it seems that packing is more difficult, but it doesn't need to be (see the Appendix). We live in a time of such relative abundance that our major packing difficulty seems to be to avoiding bringing too much gear with us.

Interest in the Camino de Santiago, and making a pilgrimage along its route, has waxed and waned over the centuries. In David M. Gitlitz and Linda Kay Davidson's rich and scholarly *The Pilgrimage Road to Santiago*, we learn that by the mid-10th century, making the pilgrimage was becoming an established tradition. By the 11th and 12th century, the number of pilgrims traveling the Camino was at its zenith: perhaps half a million per year. Interest remained high during the Middle Ages, but dropped during the Renaissance.

It has, however, never completely stopped. We are once again seeing an upswing in interest and travel on the Camino. When Gitlitz and Davidson made their first trek in 1974, they met no other pilgrims; when they returned in 1979, they met only one. In 1987 and 1993, they met hundreds.

ANOTHER WAY OF gauging interest in the Camino is by the books that have been published about it. The first known guide to the Camino, attributed by many to Aymery Picaud, was within the set of five books collectively known as the *Codex Calixtinus*. These five books were published in the 12th century.

The books included sermons on St. James, hymns and lessons for his feast days, stories of his miracles and legends, an epic tale of Charlemagne in Spain, and music of the polyphonic style (having many tones or voices).

THE *CODEX CALIXTINUS* reads that pilgrims were promised "the absence of evils, immortality of the flesh, an increase in virtues, forgiveness of sins, repentance to those doing penance, the right-minded way, the love of the saints, belief in the Resurrection, a prize to the blessed, drawing away from Hell, and receiving the protection of Heaven.

"A pilgrimage also distances us from tempting delicacies, keeps in check the fleshly desires that attack the bastion of the soul, cleanses the spirit, invites the person to a life of contemplation, humbles the proud, ennobles the low-born, and cherishes poverty."

Book Five was an invaluable guide to the earlier traveler. It provided information about the trail's route: the terrain, the climate, descriptions of the towns, and where to seek food and lodging. It also gave colorful descriptions of the townspeople and tales of some of the unsavory highwaymen.

> "The water of all rivers one encounters between Estella and Logroño has been recognized as deadly for the men and the horses that drink from it, and their fish is no less dangerous to eat. Should you anywhere in Spain or in Galicia eat either the fish vulgarly called barbo, or the one those of Poinou call *alose* and the Italian *clipia*, or even the eel or the tenca, you will no doubt die shortly thereafter or at least fall sick. And if somebody by chance ate them without falling sick, this is either because he was healthier than most, or because he had stayed in the country for a long time. All fish and the meat of beef and pork from all of Spain and Galicia cause sickness to foreigners."
>
> —*Codex Calixtinus, Chapter VI* (translation by Melczer, pg. 89)

DURING THE 14TH, 15th, and 16th centuries, scores of books by and for travelers coming from throughout Europe to make a pilgrimage were published. More recently the trail's notoriety and visitation by Americans increased when Shirley MacLaine wrote *The Camino: A Journey of the Spirit*, an account of her 1994 walk. When it was published in 2000, it quickly became a best seller.

....NOW RALPH AND I were ready for our own Camino journey....

MADRID JOURNAL, DAY 1 (Wednesday, August 29, 2001): **San Francisco to Madrid. Travel.**

RALPH AND I flew from San Francisco to Madrid on August 29, 2001. Up at five-fifteen AM, piled into the airporter at five forty-five. Flight left SFO at nine AM (on time!), arrived New York's Kennedy at three-fifteen PM. Went directly to Iberia Airlines, which flies non-stop to Madrid. Left New York at six-forty (EST time) to arrive at Madrid seven-fifteen AM Thursday. The total flight time was twelve hours, but we were in transit for seventeen.

The segment with American Airlines was great. The seats were comfortable and had plenty of legroom. There were only two seats on each side, so we could trade our window and aisle seats whenever we wanted and making it easy to get in and out. On top of that, we had a funny movie. The Iberia portion was more cramped: three seats on the side. It felt much more claustrophobic, and I had to worry about disturbing the person on the aisle (who actually was quite gracious about me doing so). The airplane was also a lot noisier.

MADRID JOURNAL, DAY 2 (Thursday, August 30): **Hotel Paris, Madrid.**

AFTER LANDING AT Barajas Airport at seven-fifteen AM, we located a bus to take us to Colon Square in the heart of Madrid. From there, we walked, wearing our backpacks, about 12 blocks to our hotel. Though we could've taken a taxi, we chose to walk because we had been sitting so long and wanted to get used to carrying our stuff.

We checked into the incongruously named Hotel Paris. We'd given ourselves two nights to recover from jet lag and to visit the fine museums of the city. (Madrid, as it turned out, was the only place where we made reservations ahead of time.)

The hotel is fine; it's clean and is reasonably quiet because it overlooks the inner courtyard rather than facing the busy streets. (The fan will probably have to run all night because the temperature is in the 70s–80s.) Though the rooms are rather plain with unadorned walls, there are parquet floors. We have a bidet; I'm looking forward to trying it.

We had lunch early. It took a while to figure out the menu, but I ended up with paella and a salad of iceberg lettuce, un-ripe tomatoes, and hard-boiled egg. We finished our drinks and then went back for a two-hour siesta. It was really hard to get up again.

WE WENT TO the section east of Old Madrid known as *Bourbon Madrid*. Carlos III (one of the Bourbon monarchs) built squares with fountains, a gateway, and a museum. The gardens are now named Parque del Retiro. Some of the world's finest museums are here. We went first to visit the Museo Nacional Centro de Arte Reina Sofia, a museum of twentieth century art with significant works by Picasso, Miró, and Dali. The museum, built in the late 1700s, was once the General Hospital.

The most important work at the National Museum is Picasso's *Guernica*. Originally Picasso was commissioned to paint a mural to be hung in the 1937 Paris Expo. With *Guernica*, Picasso meant to awaken neutral world powers to the atrocities occurring under Spain's General Franco's fascist regime and to gather support for the Republicans during the Spanish Civil War.

GUERNIKA (AKA GERNIKA-LUMO) is a small Basque village where Basque leaders had met for centuries in a democratic fashion. On April 26, 1937, on a busy market day, Franco ordered a major bombing raid on the town. More than one thousand civilians died. Picasso began painting *Guernica*, an eleven-foot-six-inch by twenty-five-foot-eight-inch mural of blacks, whites, and grays of grotesque figures and dark symbols, as protest.

"I am not interested in painting to decorate apartments," Picasso adamantly told one interviewer. He demanded

Guernica be kept out of Spain until democracy was reestablished. He himself never returned to Spain. The mural hung in the New York Museum of Modern Art for many years. After Franco's death in 1975, Spain's political system changed again. A general election was held in 1982 and Felipe Gonzalez was elected. *Guernica* was returned to Spain, where it was displayed first at the famous Prado Museum, then moved to the National Museum in 1992.

JOURNAL, DAY 2, resumes: I know we were supposed to love visiting the museum. Unfortunately, I was too tired to appreciate all that I was seeing. I did much better when we were outside. Wearing our packs again so we'd be in better condition for the long hiking days ahead we walked to the central plaza, the Plaza Mayor, the largest of Madrid. It's hard to imagine it as the scene of the Inquisitions. The plaza is now surrounded by various government buildings, shops, and restaurants.

We sat at one of the outdoor tables and enjoyed a beer. Then we headed back towards our hotel and stumbled upon a wonderful *pasteleria* (bakery). I selected a rich, buttery apple turnover and a Diet Coke and took them back to the hotel and read for a while.

Then we forced ourselves to go out again hoping to get into the local time. Since it was approaching the dinner hour, the streets were now filled with people. We walked through the crowded streets until after dark, then returned to our hotel and fell into bed, exhausted pilgrims. We'd had only two hours sleep in the last thirty hours.

MADRID, AS IS the case in most large European cities, really comes to life late at night. While there, you are hard-pressed to find anywhere to eat dinner earlier than nine PM. The nightclubs and dance spots generally don't open until eleven, and don't hit their max until two in the morning.

It wasn't long before we realized that adjusting our internal clocks to Spain's time zone was not going to be the only time factor to consider. No sooner would we adjust to what I'll call "Madrid Time" then we were going to have to adapt to the time schedules of the refugios. "Camino Time" would be entirely different; we'd read that many refugios locked their doors by ten and expected travelers to be gone by eight the next morning.

MADRID JOURNAL, DAY 3 (Fri. Aug. 31): **Hotel Paris, Madrid.**

OUR BED, CAMA *matrimonial*, is a standard double bed with one unusual feature: it has one long pillow for the two of us. At home I'm used to being able to turn my pillow over to get to the cool side, but with the shared one here, it's impossible. However, no doubt from exhaustion, I slept well anyway. We woke at eight and went down for breakfast. The hotel's fare (included in our $75 a night rate) was good: a crisp French roll with butter and jam, an apple-filled pastry with powdered sugar, an orange drink, and tea or coffee.

We walked to *The Museo de Prado* (Prado Museum), which is considered one of the world's finest art museums.

The Prado opened in 1819 to display the royal collection of paintings, sculpture, and decorative arts dating from the 12th to the 19th centuries. Its *Cason del Buen Retiro,* an annex that is behind the primary museum, has art from the 19th and 20th centuries.

The Prado's collection of Spanish art, as well as that of Italian and Flemish artists, is superb. Its collections reflect the wealth and power that Spain held from the late 1400s to the late 1600s. Works not to be missed include that of such masters as Velazquez, Goya, El Greco, Rubens, Rembrandt, and Botticelli.

JOURNAL RESUMES: WE saw the work of the famous El Greco. The museum is huge; my feet were soon killing me and I was feeling exhausted. Still, we were determined to see all that we could in our short time here. We both prefer Impressionist to Classical art, so after lunch we returned to the *Paseo del Prado* (the walkway nearby) to visit the *Museo Thyssen-Bornemisza*. (The Thyssen-Bornemisza Museum is named for Baron Heinrich Thyssen. The Baron and his son, Baron Hans Heinrich, collected its world-famous art.)

Though the Museo Thyssen-Bornemisza has work of earlier periods, including paintings by Rubens and Titian, we spent most of our time enjoying the Impressionist and modern art. The collection included paintings by Pissarro, O'Keefe, Van Gogh, Manet, as well as Jasper Johns, Jason Pollock, and Miró.

We took a siesta from four to six, then found an outdoor restaurant. For the first course, Ralph played it safe by ordering gazpacho. I had a "Russian" salad, which turned out to be made primarily of potatoes. I ordered pork even though it made me nervous to see the whole roasted pig sitting on display. But my serving of pork was slices—no snout or trotters. The veggies were overcooked—at least to one used to California cuisine with its emphasis on *al dente*: the artichoke had been cooked to the point where it fell apart and had lost most of its delicate flavor. The pastries, however, were great. I enjoyed a *pain au chocolat* (flaky, layered pastry filled with chocolate).

Our hotel has a lot of college-age kids. Their excitement, on top of the energy of the city, is contagious. Our train leaves at eight tomorrow morning for a five-hour ride to Pamplona.

THE HECTIC PACE of Madrid made our stay there a blur. As we explored Madrid, I tried to be "in the moment" and experience this wondrous Iberian metropolis, but always in the back of my mind were questions about the upcoming journey. Each morning, I'd awaken with a sense of both excitement and trepidation; "What lies ahead?" "Can I do it?"

Walking Through the Pyrenees.

REGION 1
THE PYRENEES

Region 1 – The Pyrenees – Some Distances

- St. Jean-Pied-de-Port to Santiago   480 miles
- St. Jean to Roncesvalles   16 miles
- Roncesvalles to Zubiri   13.5 miles
- Zubiri to Trinidad de Arre   11 miles
- Trinidad to Pamplona   2.5 miles

The Pyrenees viewed from the pilgrimage route in southern France, ninety miles from St. Jean-Pied-de-Port.

1 • Roncesvalles to Zubiri

On Foot in the Pyrenees

*As for courage and will—we can not measure how much of
each lies within us, we can only trust there will be sufficient to
carry through trials which may lie ahead.*

—Andre Norton

CAMINO JOURNAL, DAY 1 (Saturday, September 1, 2001): **Madrid to Roncesvalles.**

OUR LAST MORNING in Madrid had somewhat of a shaky start because I had hardly slept. My neck hurt, and my ears would not clear; they had been popping ever since our take-off from SFO. And our wake-up call came at six-thirty: too early for breakfast.

The taxi picked us up at seven for our short ride to the train station. That much was easy, but once at the station we had to figure out where to board the train. Seating was scheduled for seven-thirty. We finally located the flashing sign indicating our train, and climbed aboard. The seats were comfortable, though not reclining. I was disappointed that instead of being seated together, Ralph and I were both on the aisle, one behind the other. I had wanted to watch the scenery, but the man seated next to me slept for two hours with the curtain drawn, so I could see very little.

Luckily after that initial period, the man next to me departed, and so did Ralph's *ventana* (window) person, so I moved up and could see the pretty countryside the rest of the way. Madrid is dry; the closer we got to Pamplona the denser the vegetation became.

WE ARRIVED IN Pamplona at twelve-fifty, then took a bus. Ralph knew just what bus to take to the center of town (#9) and we got right to the center of town and the autobus terminal. There were many bus lines, which was really confusing, with no posted schedule for where we were going, but fortunately we found another passenger who could tell us what was going on.

We went for lunch: more confusion. We finally managed to order a ham (more like thick bacon) and pepper sandwich, beer and dessert. We returned to the bus station to wait.

The bus soon arrived. The only reason we knew it was the right one was that there was a sudden flurry of activity as all the backpackers started moving toward it. We found out that it was going to leave at four in the afternoon. We climbed on. The bus was soon full; it was not yet three-thirty and many anxious travelers were still waiting outside. The bus line somehow came up with a second bus and everyone managed to catch a ride. I was glad to be on board; the woman at a neighboring ticket counter had told us the bus left at six. I wondered what happened to anyone who arrived later expecting a six o'clock departure.

The ride from Pamplona to Roncesvalles was beautiful. The road became increasingly curvy as it wound its way through many hamlets on our climb into the Pyrenees. The two-storied houses were well cared for with freshly-painted white plaster exteriors. Their curved red-tile roofs, crisply-painted flower boxes, and pots filled with red geraniums were picture-book perfect.

WE ARRIVED IN the tiny hamlet of Roncesvalles at five PM; it had been a long day. The bus stopped near the dark Gothic church, which has welcomed pilgrims since the twelfth century. We hoped

to stay in the *refugio* (hostel) in the church's monastery.
Everyone began scrambling out of buses and getting in a long line. For what, we had no idea. We followed the crowd. No one was speaking English; we had to piece together overheard bits of conversations. It turned out that the line was to get a credential: the folding paper document that we were to carry with us to indicate that we're pilgrims on the walk to Santiago. Though we knew we were in the correct line to obtain the credencial (credential or pilgrim's passport), I was still anxious; we had no idea whether or not we had a place to stay that night.

We waited outside the dark-colored, closed doors of a large room. We watched as groups of about sixteen at a time were invited in. When we were admitted, we filed in, took a seat at a long table, which had printed forms in place and pens fastened with cords to the table. The woman in charge rattled off instructions in Spanish. She repeated them in Spanish, but then in English when we asked. "Bed by ten PM, out by eight AM, order dinner ahead of time to eat dinner at the nearby restaurant at eight-thirty," she sternly announced.

AFTER EVERYONE IN line was registered, the real chaos began. The woman took everyone into the refuge in an adjoining building. Dark, old, flights of stairs, numerous rooms. As she was giving directions, people started grabbing thick mats from a stack to sleep on; the first room filled quickly. Directions continued, other rooms filled up.

I grabbed a mat and tried to find a place to put it on the floor. Heads shook, "no room, full." I couldn't even find a place to put a mat! Finally, a couple of women realized that Ralph and I didn't have a clue to what was going on, took pity, moved things around, and offered me a place. I didn't know what was happening with Ralph, if they would make room for him, or what. I sank to the mat, my stomach in a knot, struggled to hold back the tears that would have been embarrassing to release.

Then just as I thought I might survive the night, a woman came to get us and indicated that we were to follow her. "Where are we going now?" I wondered. Though the guidebook stated that the refugio held less than sixty, I was certain there were at least a hundred people there.

We went up two flights of winding stairs. We ended up with two upper bunks and on adjoining bunks. The guy in the bunk below me dragged a bench over so I could get up and down more easily. I climbed up. I pondered silently how old I'd been when I last had slept in a bunk bed: perhaps eight or ten years old? I tried not to think about the prospect of falling out of the skinny bunk during the middle of the night.

With that traumatizing introduction to Spanish communal living, and because the monastery is set in a small valley and by late afternoon was fairly dark and dreary, we were a little apprehensive about how things were going to go. However, we set out to explore the town. Besides the refugio, church, the restaurant (which also had rooms for rent), and a shop that sold some flavorful cheeses, wines, breads, and souvenirs, there was little else. We bought some olive bread for lunches ahead.

Dinner was very good. It was served at two seatings; we went to the one at eight-thirty. For 1,000 *pesetas* (about $6) we had a thick broth with pasta that was warm and filling followed by fresh trout, wine, bread, and ice cream; having a little food and wine improved our mood. Then to bed. I took a sleeping pill and slept well.

OVER THE NEXT few days, we learned a lot more about how refugios worked and where we would find food along the way.

Ralph and I began our hike in Roncesvalles where the routes over the Pyrenees from St. Jean-Pied-de-Port converge and the trail works its way down out of the mountains. Roncesvalles is a tiny hamlet, dominated by a monastery. Pilgrims have been welcomed here dating back to the 12th century. Originally the monks of the abbey helped travelers; nowadays, D. Javier Navarro and a group of volunteers assist.

Like most villages along the Camino, Roncesvalles has its own claim to fame. This is the area where Charlemagne, King of the Franks (French), retreated into France in 778. The legend is that when Charlemagne's rearguard was ambushed, the French knight Roland blew his horn to summon the emperor and his heroic actions were instrumental in stopping the Muslims from further invasions. (Roland's bravery later inspired the epic poem, *Song of Roland*.)

MOST TRAVELERS WHO plan to travel the entire length of the Camino de Santiago start at St. Jean-Pied-de-Port, which is on the French side of the French/Spanish border, *or* at Roncesvalles, which is just over the crest of the Pyrenees in Spain. The hike from St. Jean-Pied-de-Port to Roncesvalles is about sixteen miles (25.76 km) through the Pyrenees, and a cumulative ascent of 4,500 ft. (1,371 m.).

Pilgrims traveling from St. Jean-Pied-de-Port have two routes from which to choose: the *Route Napoléon* and the route that generally follows the highway (Spanish N135) and passes through the town of Valcarlos. The first, *Route Napoléon*, is more dramatic but also more strenuous and potentially more hazardous. When the weather is clear, the views of the Pyrenees and back to St. Jean-Pied-de-Port are spectacular. Sightings of birds of prey and deer are frequent.

The *Route Napoléon* follows minor roads and unpaved trails. The pass is 3,565 ft. (1,087 m.) in elevation and although it is much lower than the highest point in the Pyrenees, which is far south at Picos de Aneto (11,165 ft./3,404 m.), even here high winds, bitter cold, fog, and avalanches are quite possible. In some years, snow may fall as early as September and the pass can be covered with snow until the following summer.

When following the *Route Napoléon*, hikers and cyclists will reach Col de Lepoeder—where medieval pilgrims would typically plant a wooden cross and pray for a safe journey—and once again have a two routes from which to choose. The alternatives for the last few kilometers downhill to Roncesvalles are the old Roman route or the Puerta de Ibañeta. The Roman route is shorter, but steeper, and less well marked. The route via Puerta de Ibañeta is longer, but more gradual. (Puerta de Ibañeta is the actual spot where Charlemagne heard Roland's horn signaling for help.)

THE ALTERNATE ROUTE from St. Jean, through Valcarlos, primarily follows roads. It traverses the mountains at lower elevations. In medieval times, pilgrims generally followed this more hospitable route, but some chose the more mountainous *Route Napoléon* because it was less frequented by bandits. The route through Valcarlos is recommended whenever taking the *Route Napoléon* might be hazardous because of inclement weather, or any time when a less strenuous route is desired. On either route, even during the summer, it is not uncommon for travelers to encounter short, but substantial, downpours.

JOURNAL, DAY 2 (Sunday, September 2): **Roncesvalles to Zubiri (13.5 miles/22 km).**

OUR HIKE HAS begun. At seven-thirty this morning, we tied our scallop shells to the front of our backpacks, lifted the fifteen-pound packs onto our backs, and officially set foot on the Camino. I imagine most people would feel pretty excited about what lies ahead. I felt a combination of things: excitement and curiosity about starting on an unknown journey and anxiety and concern about whether I had the stamina for the long trek ahead. We soon encountered two men in traditional pilgrim garb (including the heavy cloaks). They also wore, as does almost everyone who walks the Camino, the symbolic scallop shell on their backpacks.

In about three kilometers we hit Burguete, a favorite fishing site for Ernest Hemingway. Its hostel boasts a piano with his signature. We noticed that the town was also known as Auritz and found out that all the towns on this part of the trail have a Basque name as well as a Spanish one.

We found a restaurant that served hot beverages and croissants. After placing our order for my tea and Ralph's coffee, we selected two bananas from the woven basket next to the register. We let our backpacks slide to the floor and sat down at a nearby table to enjoy our breakfast. We ate quickly so that we could get back on the trail. On the way out of town, we stopped briefly at a *panaderia* (bakery) to purchase a hearty-looking loaf of rye bread and some salami, cheese, and orange juice for lunch. Finally, we felt ready for the day.

The Scallop Shell

In the Middle Ages, those returning from their pilgrimage to Santiago de Compostela wore a scallop shell that they had found or purchased while there. The western coast of Galicia (the district within which Santiago de Compostela is located) is on the Atlantic Ocean and therefore scallop shells were easily obtained. Pilgrims attached the shell to their hat or pouch and it announced that they indeed were *peregrinos* (pilgrims). Once in Santiago, however, their trip was only halfway completed; they had to return home much as they had come.

Nowadays, most pilgrims *begin* their journey with a scallop shell (which they tie to their backpack) because most walk west, but return home by modern transportation. The origin of this custom of wearing the scallop shell dates back to the time when the stone boat carrying James's body approached the Galician coast. According to legend, as the boat neared shore, a young man on horseback leaped off the cliff at Cape Finisterre and into the sea. Miraculously, the man and his horse rose to the surface, covered with scallop shells, and swam alongside the boat to shore. From that time onward the scallop shell has been associated with St. James and the pilgrimage to Santiago.

Today the scallop shell is widely used as a symbol of the Camino; it's seen on road signs and trail markers as well as on the official *credencial* (a passport) that pilgrims carry.

Refugios (also called *albergues*) have provided accommodations to pilgrims from the earliest times. In those times, the names used were commonly *hospital, hospice,* and *monastery.* Nowadays we think of a hospital as being a place to seek medical care, not a place to stay overnight. In earlier times, there was considerable overlap: hospitals provided not only medical assistance to local residents and travelers, but also bed and board to healthy pilgrims. The quality of medical care was wide-ranging. Eldor Pederson, who frequently contributes to the GoCamino forum, writes, "In a small village, the hospital might provide what we would now term first aid given by a kindly, but untrained, monk or nun. In the larger hospitals, 'state of the art' treatment was provided by physicians trained in great universities such as those of Bologna, Paris, or Salamanca."

Nowadays there are pilgrim refugios every nine to fifteen miles along the route to Santiago, where pilgrims can stay overnight. Usually a nominal fee is charged; if it is not, a donation should be given. A refugio nowadays is a dormitory reserved exclusively for the use of pilgrims traveling the Camino on foot, bicycle, or horseback.

The seasons and hours that they are open are varied; the *Pilgrim Guide* will be very important because it gives these details. When pilgrims arrive at each refugio, their *credencial* will be checked to make sure that they are entitled to use the facilities, then stamped and returned.

IN EARLIER TIMES, travelers arriving at a hospice would generally find a sleeping room with one large straw mattress all to be shared with a dozen or so companions. Nowadays, refugios offer a less rudimentary stay; however, it is wise to expect no more than a clean place to throw down your sleeping bag and to be thrilled when you find more.

Usually the sleeping rooms are co-ed. The quality of the accommodations varies; some have hot water at all hours, kitchens, and washer and dryer. Others have cold water and concrete floors. Most often they will be somewhere in between: with beds, feeble water flow in the showers, electricity, washtubs, and clotheslines.

Churches, charities, municipalities, and occasionally families, run refugios. Oftentimes the people who maintain the facility are volunteers. Cleanliness also varies both because of the staff and the recent travelers.

Because August is the peak month for pilgrims on the Camino, and July is second, the refugios are most crowded during those months. Traditionally accommodations have been strictly first come, first served: no reservations taken. However, because of growing concern about overcrowding, there is currently discussion of imposing small fees and allowing reservations to be made in the Galician municipal-run refugios.

Precedence is usually given to pilgrims who arrive on foot, then bicycle, then horseback, but with the increasing strain on the system, this isn't always enforced. We didn't carry a sleeping pad, but if we were to hike during the summer months again, we would probably carry them to eliminate the worry that we'd arrive late and have to sleep on the floor.

THERE IS A daily routine: generally the refugios want everyone out by eight in the morning; some people start getting up and out by five. We found ourselves caught up in a "refugio mentality": get off to an early start; hurry to get to the next place before all the beds fill up.

Because things would start stirring so early in the morning and because of the snoring, earplugs are essential. Even so, we found ourselves becoming a little sleep-deprived. About every fourth day we would check into a small hotel for recovery.

We met very few English speakers along the way. We found it difficult to communicate in the refugios because we didn't know French or German—or even Spanish as spoken in Spain. Even though we have traveled a fair amount in Mexico, we were dismayed to find that it was much harder for us to acquire an "ear" for Spanish as it is spoken along the Camino. Not only is some of the vocabulary different, but also some of the pronunciation. For example instead of the "c" sound that we use in "cent," we heard "c" pronounced as "th." Therefore, "cinco" becomes "think-o."

IT WOULD BE worthwhile for visitors to learn the variants before their trip (Lonely Planet's *Walking in Spain* has a helpful vocabulary section). We had sufficient Spanish to get food and shelter, but found it hard to carry on meaningful conversations. Nevertheless we made friends along the way: sometimes because people spoke English and sometimes by getting a third party to translate.

JOURNAL, DAY 2, *resumes:* The villages of the Pyrenees are colorful with a freshly-scrubbed prosperous look. Our trail went through wooded hills with beech trees, yarrow, honeysuckle, blackberries, heather, and gorse. We came upon a violet flower with no leaves that we couldn't positively identify, but we assumed was a crocus). I later read in Davies and Cole's *Walking the Camino de Santiago* that the beech forest surrounding Roncesvalles is the only site in Europe in which all seven species of European woodpecker can be found.

   The trail was generally good, with well-tamped rock or dirt, or paved with rounded stones; all of these surfaces are kinder to the feet than hard concrete or flat asphalt. Some stretches were well-weathered; others washed-out from earlier rains. Overall we descended, but we had some uphill stretches, too. Most of all, I liked the level areas along the ridgeline.

   We passed, and were passed, often by the same people, as alternately we stopped to eat, shed a jacket, or otherwise take a break. Spanish seemed to come more easily today, or at least we were able to communicate better. We enjoyed our salami sandwiches.

I suspect that today's long hours of studying the pastoral landscape and seeing little else but hundreds of cows and sheep is addling my brain. So, it should come as no surprise that I came up with a creative, albeit ridiculous, idea for a new book, *Why Cows Paint*. It would be similar to Heather Busch's *Why Cats Paint*, except that my book would be illustrated with drawings similar to the varied cow pies we've seen. The way I envision it, Ralph and I, in order to gather material for the book, would be forced to travel around the world studying the differences in cow droppings. *Why Cows Paint* would become an instant success much as Pet Rocks, Chia pets, and Silly Putty were in their day.

Alternative Accommodations

Though the emphasis here is on the *refugios* (refuges) or *albergues* for pilgrims along the Camino, there may well be times when travelers would prefer alternative accommodations. It could be that the *refugio* is full, that they prefer to camp outdoors for a while, or that they'd like the comfort, privacy, and hot showers provided in a private room. Spain's official designations of various categories of accommodations are:

- *Campgrounds* (three levels) are known as *campings*. They charge a fee, generally have hot showers and a store. During the peak months in July and August, popular campgrounds will be packed like sardine cans, but they can generally pack in one more tent. An area where one can pitch a tent (but usually without sanitary facilities) is called a *Zona de acampada* or *area de acampadao*. If hikers decide to camp on private land they should ask the permission of the landowner first.

- *Albergues juveniles* (youth-hostels) are inexpensive for singles, but a couple may find the hostels' prices to be the same as other facilities that offer more for the money. If travelers have youth-hostel passes from home, they should carry them because many places will honor other countries' passes and give a lower rate. Youth-hostels do not require that their patrons be either a hostel member, or a juvenile, to stay in these rooms.

- *Pensiones* are small, private hotels that are usually run by a family. They can be recognized by their sign with a "P" on blue background. Prices vary: one factor being whether the bathroom is "en suite" or down the hall. Pensiones offer the opportunity to experience Spain in a more intimate way than hotels provide on tourist routes. Meals may be included. Although Spain no longer officially designates these categories, one can generally be guided by *Fonda* (a white "F" on the sign) and *Casa de Huespedes* ("CH") to alternate accommodations offering simple rooms, shared bathrooms, and low rates.
- *Hostales* are rated by a three-star system. They offer rooms ranging from where pensiones leave off to quite comfortable accommodations with a bathroom in every room.
- *Casa Rurales* are a relatively recent type of lodging. Similar to Bed & Breakfast rooms in England and the United States, *Casa Rurales* are homes in town, or farmhouses in the country, where bedrooms have been converted to guest rooms. Some offer meals, others sleeping accommodations only.
- *Hotels* are rated by a five-star system; five-star hotels are expected to provide fine service and unique characteristics. *Gran Lujo* (Grand Luxury) hotels are the best of the best.
- *Paradores* are hotels within a state-run system. Spain has 86 paradores; they're hotels that were formerly castles, palaces, or monasteries and so forth of historic note. They are usually in areas of great beauty and offer a unique opportunity to experience the elegance of Spain. Accommodations vary but they generally rate three or four stars. Some paradores offer rooms in buildings adjoining the original building. So ask whether or not the room offered is in the historic building when making a reservation. Many paradores offer discounts to people 60 years old or more. Ask about the "Dias Dorados." Contact: Paradores de Turismo, Velazquez, 18, 28001 Madrid. Tel: (91) 435 9700 or (91) 435 9744.
- *Other* options are more appropriate for those planning a lengthier stay: apartments and spa/health resorts. Both of these alternatives are generally arranged by travel agents.

Obtaining food and drink is not a problem while on the Camino, but sometimes it takes a bit of planning, particularly for breakfast. Though most villages have a bar, which is where food is generally available, they usually are not open by eight when the hungry hiker is trying to find breakfast. So, most mornings one has to walk a couple of hours to the next village, stop for coffee or tea and a croissant, and then walk on.

In Spain, towns large and small have a public fountain where pilgrims can fill their water bottles. And after several hours of hot trudging, these towns are a welcome sight. With few exceptions, and signs will indicate this, water from the fountains does not need any treatment.

IT TOOK US a couple of days to come up with a plan for our lunches. We didn't want to eat in restaurants every afternoon; we preferred to carry sandwich-makings. It was less expensive and often more convenient because we could stop whenever we were hungry rather than being dependent on finding an open restaurant. We usually shopped for bread, salami, fruit and hard cheese in the evening in order to have provisions for our picnics for the next few days.

When it was time to shop again, we sometimes checked our guidebook, but often as not, we kept our eyes open and found a market on our own. Sometimes stores aren't marked, but there will be produce outside of what looks like a home. The custom is to knock on the door and negotiate with the vendor. We quickly learned another of the local customs: customers are expected to point to the pieces of fruit that they want and allow the storekeeper to pick up the items and put them in the bag.

If we were not carrying a picnic lunch, we usually stopped for a mid-day break at a bar. A bar in Spain is much more than a place that serves liquor. Aside from the church, it's the social center of the town. Bars serve food and excellent coffee, and provide a place to exchange information and conduct business. The town elderly, rather than being shut away, are quietly sitting in the bar, enjoying the activity. We enjoyed watching the locals as we rested our hot and weary bodies, quenched our thirst, and scarfed down a *bocadillo* (half a baguette, commonly stuffed with cheese and ham, sausage, or salami).

FOR MOST PILGRIMS, dinner is a highlight of the day. Though some refugios have kitchens for pilgrim use, there most likely will be many opportunities to eat out. In the evening many bars and restaurants offer *menú del dia* (or *el menú*, it's the "menu of the day"). For a very reasonable price, substantial courses are served (from a limited number of choices): soup or salad, entree, and dessert. Usually a full bottle or carafe of house wine will accompany the meal. Restaurants typically do not serve dinner until eight-thirty or after.

JOURNAL, DAY 2, resumes: The last couple of hours were the hardest—downhill, rutted, hot miles—but we managed to reach the refugio about three-thirty in the afternoon. We both ended up with top bunks again. I still don't like taking one, but I'm adapting. I think just knowing the routines helps somewhat. A cool shower was delightful, and changing to non-sweaty clothes and having a good dinner made it all better.

We had intended to get the pilgrim menu (a low cost meal), but we couldn't find the restaurant in town that offered it. We paid $30 for our meal, but it was worth it. We enjoyed vegetable soup, followed by the main course (spaghetti with a fish sauce with a few shrimp), red wine, bread, and dessert. The dessert was similar to pound cake, but with nuts added and soaked with *pacharan* (a liqueur of sloe berries and sweet aniseed). It's a regional, and delicious, treat.

I guess consuming a half carafe of red wine was a bit too much for me. When we were leaving, I tried to open the door to the outside, but to no avail. It turned out it wasn't the exit. After watching me fumble around for a while with the door to a closet, Ralph told me I'd provided entertainment enough for the waitress. Apparently the wine *does* have the standard alcohol content; I was feeling *really* good.

The Basque

Our hike across Spain began in Basque country (*Euskedi* in Euskara, the Basque language). The Basque country within Spain is composed of three provinces. Two, Bizkaia and Gipuzkoa, are on the Atlantic, and one Araba/Alaba is inland. The Navarra region is autonomous in the Spanish system, but shares ties with the Basque regions. Fishing and trade have traditionally supported the regions on the coast. It is a land of mountains, valleys, cliffs and forests. Primarily the land is limestone in composition, with the exception of granite areas near San Sebastian.

The Basques of the interior have traditionally supported themselves in both urban and rural settings. Though sheep herding has diminished as an economic factor, there are still many who tend flocks in the traditional style. Cows (providing milk and meat) and horses (whose meat the French and Italians enjoy) also graze on the hillside and bring in needed cash.

The Basque farmhouse, *baserria,* generally has three stories: the ground level for sheltering cows, hens, and the farm implements, the second level for the family, and the third level for storing hay and corn. The top and ground-level floors help insulate the family's living quarters, which is an important consideration in these lands of heavy rainfall.

Though Spanish is spoken by the Basques in Spain, many still use *Euskara* also. Linguists say that *Euskara* is a unique language, sharing nothing with other known languages, and may date back to the Stone Age. Highway signs, as well as other official signs, show both languages.

To many, the mention of Basque brings thoughts of political strife. The separatist organization of ETA, *Euzkadi ta Azkatauna,* claims they are pressing for a Basque state carved out of northern Spain and southwestern France. The United States and the European Union call them terrorists.

Whether or not one labels them as such, they do have a violent history. Since their beginnings in the 1960s, they have engaged in such minor disruptions as burning trash in barrels in cities to major crimes, including assassination, against members of opposition parties, police, and military personnel. French and Spanish police have arrested hundreds of ETA suspects in recent years, severely weakening the organization

Still, in August 2004, following five months of relative quiet after the train bombings in Madrid, two small explosions were set off: one in Santiago de Compostela and another in the nearby city of La Coruna. A telephone warning had been made to a newspaper. The ETA claimed credit. No one was injured, but it reminds us that the wise visitor will be alert to demonstrations.

Bridge of the Magdalena as you enter Pamplona.

2 • Zubiri to Cizur Menor

Starting to Get the Hang of It

I wanted to live deep and suck out all the marrow of life...
—Henry David Thoreau

JOURNAL, DAY 3 (Monday, September 3): **Zubiri to Trinidad de Arre (11 miles/18 km).**

WE WERE AWAKENED at six by everyone else packing up and starting out to get a jump on the limited accommodations in Pamplona (100 beds), which is about 14 miles from here. Since we were stopping short of there (here in Trinidad de Arre), we didn't have to hurry. I wanted to roll over and continue sleeping, but of course I didn't have that luxury.

We left Zubiri about seven-thirty. It was too early to find anyplace open for breakfast, but we had a bit of granola bar (that I had insisted we bring despite Ralph's protests because of its weight). The day was bright and beautiful, and we started down through a deciduous forest on the trail—once we located it. The Camino is well marked, mainly by splashes of yellow paint on rocks, on buildings, and on street signs, but it takes some getting used to.

By nine, we had reached the next village, Larrasoaña, and found a place to eat. Luckily, custard-filled pastries were among the breakfast items available and they went a long way towards

31

making up for the lateness of breakfast.

Last night, once again, I couldn't sleep. At first it was because my stomach was upset. I took some Pepto Bismol, but then kept tasting it in my throat. Next, I started feeling too warm. I had to get up twice to pee, but each time I waited and worried about the unstable ladder I'd have to use to climb up and down. I was eventually forced out of my bunk by nature's call, which outweighed my trepidation. I wanted to take another sleeping pill, but decided against it because the doctor had advised me not to take them too often as "they're addictive." (Since I hadn't asked for clarification, and didn't know what "too often" meant, I made my own rule that I wouldn't take them two nights in a row.)

About three AM, after checking my watch for the umpteenth time, I decided to pass the time by telling my life story to myself. An hour later, just about the time I reached the beginning of the seventh-grade and remembered how nervous I had felt when I went to my first dance, I fell asleep.

OUR DAY'S HIKE was less up and down, but hotter and less scenic. One thing we've begun to notice is that very few old buildings are torn down. They're just added to; what was once a dwelling now becomes a stable; old stones join new. Buildings are made from the materials at hand; stone is plentiful in the Pyrenees. Most of the trail was in the open, with a stretch of about a half-mile on the shoulder of the highway, but at least there was a breeze when trucks passed. Blisters and general foot soreness are beginning to plague many hikers, including me.

Since we bought supplies at the butcher's yesterday, today's lunch break was pretty much the same as yesterday's: eating a salami and cheese sandwich while sitting on a stone wall. There were few places to sit that weren't littered with toilet paper. We'd be hiking along, look ahead and see a grassy area or a tree where it looked as if it would be pleasant to stop, and find when we got there that it was unusable. I don't like to be an "Ugly American" and complain about other countries' and cultures' ways of doing things, but it is pretty disgusting to have nowhere clean to sit. Later in the day, we stopped at a newly-built picnic area with restrooms. The signs posted indicated that locating restrooms near picnic areas was a new concept; I hope the idea spreads.

OUR REFUGIO HERE in Trinidad de Arre is in a church. The old building sitting beside the Ulzama River is quite picturesque. A huge new addition has been joined to the original small building. After we were greeted warmly, the host asked if any of us snored; those who admitted it were then condemned to their own "snoring room." The accommodations are clean. When we arrived (we were numbers five and six), we were pleased to find that we had our choice of beds. Undoubtedly the reason we were among the first here, and got a place, is that most people continue on to Pamplona, which is a better known and bigger city. The rules are typical of refugios: in by ten at night, checkout by eight in the morning

Our host gave us a quick tour of the facilities. The more we saw, the more we felt we had lucked out in our choice of accommodations. The lights are bright enough to read by. There's a *free* washing machine and dryer, a kitchen with stove and fridge, a vending machine with coffee, chocolate, and tea and so forth, and another with chips and pastries. There are also warm showers stocked with soap and shampoo. After we showered and laundered our clothes, Ralph helped me attend to my feet.

Ralph has been doing everything he can to help me. He wraps my feet in breathable, cloth tape to treat the blisters I already have and in the effort to prevent more. Also, he carries more weight in his pack to lighten my load (probably 20 pounds to my 15). But the one thing he can't do is take the steps for me; I have to take every one of those myself.

The group staying here invited us to join them for dinner. Most are French (and of course we don't speak French), but one young woman we've seen every day since the start is now translating everything for us. Anna is Spanish and lives with her family near Santiago de Compostela; she only recently graduated from college. I doubt many women on the Camino wear make-up (beyond a touch of lipstick). Anna certainly doesn't need any. Her natural beauty—olive-colored eyes, clear complexion, and dark shiny hair— doesn't need enhancement. Though she started the Camino on her own, she meets people along the way, or at the refugios, and joins her new companions for the hiking days.

While waiting for a nearby hall to open for dinner, Ralph and I sat in the central park for a half-hour. It was a treat just to sit and watch the people going about their daily affairs. Children, headed home from school, took a short-cut through the plaza. Though it was dusk, their daypacks were still heavy with textbooks. It appears that the school day is divided into two segments to accommodate the mid-day siesta. A father with his young son and daughter were there to enjoy the remaining light. While the man and his son practiced "football" (soccer to us), the girl circled on her bicycle nearby. The boy was not very good, missed the goal most of the time, but dad just calmly let him keep trying, and hit, kicked, or bumped the ball back.

JOURNAL, DAY 3, resumes: Later, another father and son of similar ages arrived; all four played a "pick-up" game. There was no yelling at the kids, just practice and patience. A group of older women gathered outside a corner building across the street to go in together for an event. Other women—some old, some young—sat on benches quietly watching or visiting as children played nearby. No televisions blared; no video games disrupted the tranquil setting (though both are prevalent in Spanish bars).

Socializing seems to be the chief entertainment in the small and medium-sized villages and towns. No one seems to be hurrying anywhere. It was very relaxing, and I watched wistfully, wishing our culture had similar settings where young, middle-aged, and old people played out intermingled and intertwined lives. The local Catholic Ladies Auxiliary had prepared the dinner. The food choices were pretty basic fare, but promised to be filling. When it came time to order the first course, we couldn't understand what was offered. We assumed all the items were vegetables, so we just picked two different things. Ralph ended up with cooked vegetables, mostly peas, so he was happy. I ended up with spaghetti.

Using our limited Spanish, we went with some safe choices for the second course: *bisteak* we knew was beefsteak and the *pollo* (chicken) was gone. We ordered the beef, and it was fine. For dessert there was a choice of a slab of vanilla ice cream or of *pina* (pineapple). We ordered the pineapple and were brought two slices. At home canned food is not our first choice for dessert, but fruit of any kind was refreshing after our several days of heavier food. We were served a whole bottle of red wine (all the wine has been good) and lots of "okay" bread (We definitely are spoiled by years of enjoying tangy San Francisco sourdough bread.)

Back at the refugio, all went well. The walls didn't reach to the ceiling, so we could hear anyone using the bathroom—which I guess would be considered amusing or disgusting, depending on one's point of view. As soon as Ralph fell asleep he started snoring, so I leapt up and shook him to make him roll over. Later, I thought he was doing it again so I got up again. It turned out it was our top bunk neighbor. Though both he and his bottom bunk companion snored through the night, it wasn't loud enough to keep me awake with my earplugs in place.

JOURNAL, DAY 4 (Tuesday, September 4): **Trinidad de Arre to Cizur Menor (5.5 miles/9 km).**

TODAY STARTED WELL. I'm beginning to feel like Bill Murray in the movie *Ground Hog Day:* experiencing each day (at least the morning's routine) as a repeat of the last one. Everyone started frantically packing at six; we left the refugio at quarter to eight, then stopped in town for pastries and coffee.

OUR ROUTE INTO Pamplona was short (about three miles) and totally paved. The elevation has dropped considerably; Pamplona is at only 1,362 feet (415 m). We crossed over the *Rio Arga* on the beautiful old stone bridge known as the *Puente de Magdalena* as we entered the beautiful city.

The entrance to the old city was spectacular: walls maybe 75 feet high, a gate with a drawbridge, narrow cobblestone streets, old stone buildings. Pamplona has been the capital of Navarra since the ninth century and was a powerful fortress city for centuries before that.

It was thrilling just to be on the street where the bulls run in the annual event immortalized by Ernest Hemingway in *The Sun Also Rises*. The street in front of the arena is named after him. Near the beautiful old town hall was a display of photographs showing hundreds of men, generally drunken, as they dashed before the charging bulls.

It would have been very exciting to have been walking the Camino at the time of the famous *Encierro* (the Running of the Bulls), but we were much too late in the year. During the July festival of *Los Sanfermines* (the festival is named for San Fermín, the first bishop of the city), Pamplona goes wild. Each morning at eight o'clock, July 7–14, a firecracker is set off to signal the beginning of the running of the bulls. Six bulls are released to run from their corral near the river, through the narrow streets of the old town, past the town hall, to the centrally located Plaza de Toros. The distance is about one-half mile (about 800 meters), so the run usually takes only a few minutes, but it can last much longer if a bull decides to turn back towards the starting point or there is some other complication. Later in the day, the bulls will fight in the arena.

RED-SCARVED MEN (WOMEN are not allowed) asserting their *machismo* run just ahead of the charging bulls. It is impossible to outrun the bulls so the runners' strategy usually involves starting out a safe distance ahead of the bulls, hanging in the race as the bulls close the gap, and making a quick escape through the double row of fencing that lines the course. Participants don't need to sign up anywhere, they just enter the run on whichever street they choose and do the best they can.

In spite of trying to keep out of harm's way, inevitably some participants are injured—an estimated forty to fifty people each year—and occasionally there's a fatality. The inherent risks of getting trampled by a 1,300-pound (600-kilos/some 120 stone) angry animal, or gored with its two big rock-hard horns while attempting to outrun it, or of getting knocked over by the crowd of drunken revelers should be carefully considered while still sober.

Tourists from around the world come not only for this exciting event but also to enjoy the other aspects of the celebration: food, wine, dancing, and parades.

JOURNAL, DAY 4, resumes: As in most cities along the Camino, Pamplona has an old section, surrounding the cathedral (*Cathedral de Santa María* in this case), and a modern city sprawling beyond. The route of the Camino invariably takes you by the cathedral.

We continued south to the University of Navarre to have our certificates stamped. As we walked through the residential section of the city, we were impressed with the ingenuity of the inverted umbrella-like structures we saw jutting out from the windows of the upper stories on narrow city streets; they're used for hanging the laundry.

Just as I was thinking I'd like to find an Internet place, I spotted a sign on a pole directing us to a shop just around the corner. It turned out to be very easy to do, 20 minutes for less than a dollar, and I was happy to be able to send messages to all.

The rest of today's hike was pretty drab, until the end. Then we caught sight of an old Romanesque church as we came into Cizur Menor, where we're staying. It's gorgeous. We're just west of Pamplona. There are two refugios in town; we chose the private one operated by the Roncal family because it is known for the hospitality of the hosts. At about four dollars, staying there was a bargain. Our building had 19 beds; some were bunks. We grabbed one set of bunk beds; for some reason, Ralph prefers being on a top one. There are curtains between groups of beds so there is more privacy than most places offer.

Our dorm was well-kept with a tiled floor, plaster walls, and dark wood-framed windows and doors. The furnishings were pleasant; the wooden beds seemed cozier than the austere metal framed ones that we've usually encountered. The small kitchen with abundant hot water was welcoming. On the wall were maps showing the route of the Camino and a profile map showing the elevations of various points along the way.

Because of the dark wood of the interior, it was still more pleasant to be outside than in. As usual we were carrying the makings for a picnic lunch, so we sat on the stone wall that surrounds the large lawn and garden and enjoyed the tranquil setting.

WE WERE IN good spirits: we'd arrived early because we'd given ourselves a short hiking day. We'd already found our beds, showered, and eaten. We needed food for the next morning's breakfast, but there was nowhere to buy food nearby. We were told that we could find a store in the neighboring village of Cizur Major, so we set out. We envisioned a charming, small village, but it turned out to be an awkwardly laid-out town with a freeway that ran along one side and then cut through the center of the town, separating the old and new sections.

We arrived at siesta time; everything in the old part of town was closed with the exception of one bar; it sold drinks and chips and little else. The one person we saw on the street spoke only Spanish. We tried asking him where to find the store we'd been told about, but we couldn't understand his directions when he gave them.

Feeling increasingly frustrated, we decided to cross on the freeway overpass to the newer section of town. Unfortunately modernization there has produced ugly, grim-looking stucco high-rise apartment buildings with little sign of habitation and lots of graffiti. All shops were closed. During the hour we wandered through the area, we saw only a handful of people. I wondered why; though both parts of town were equally empty, the old section felt as though people's absence was only temporary and in the new section their absence felt ominous.

We crossed back to the old part of town; we were determined to break the language barrier. Luckily, the young man who had tried to help us earlier was now talking with two young women. We listened carefully, watched as directions were pointed out, and set out. We finally found the area where we had been directed, but discovered that the town's only market was not due to open until five PM. Though it was almost four, the warmth of early afternoon had dissipated and it had become too cold and windy to wait.

On the way back, we encountered a Canadian woman staying at our refugio who'd made the same exploration. She, too, had returned home empty-handed. Both Ralph and I became chilled coming back, and I continued shivering even after I climbed into my sleeping bag. It was not until after I'd drunk some hot water that I felt okay again.

AT LEAST WE can have dinner in town at eight. If this entry sounds as if I'm feeling low at the moment, I've recorded my mood pretty accurately. I thought I'd done enough conditioning for this hike and that my boots were fine. It appears, however, that going on a single day's hike of 12 miles is a different story than hiking day after day with no time for the body to repair.

My boots were comfortable on the hikes we took at home; here, it seems that I start the day in comfort, but my bunions begin aching halfway through the day.

When to Make a Pilgrimage

No matter when they decide to go, those who elect to make this journey will find themselves in the company of an exciting mix of people. However, certain times of year, and certain years, are more popular than others, and for good reason. Because the Spanish section of the Camino is so lengthy, 500 miles extending from the border of France to (almost) the west coast of Spain, pilgrims can expect to encounter great variations in climate and weather depending on the region and time of year. The optimal times with regard for weather for hiking or bicycling the entire Camino are May/June or September/October.

In spring and fall the temperatures, as well as the crowds, will be reduced. In spring there'll be green fields, wildflowers blossoming, flowing rivers and creeks—and probably showers. July and August, in spite of the heat, are peak months of travel on the Camino. In large part, this is because the majority of students and teachers are out of school and most Europeans are taking their extended vacations. (See Appendix for detailed statistics.)

The fall will be harvest time; grapes will surely still be on the vine, but there will also be barren fields. October may bring rain. Since our pilgrimage was during September and October, Ralph and I made it a point to focus on the subtle differences in the golds and browns of the dry interior (the *meseta*) and the area's stark beauty.

Depending on the weather and the traveler's preparedness, winter can also be an interesting season to make a pilgrimage. The number of other people on the trail will be significantly lower than during any season, but the weather encountered will be severe, mountain passes may be blocked by snow, and many refugios and other facilities will be closed. (Read Sue Kenney's *My Camino* for the account of her winter pilgrimage.)

Another consideration when planning is that religious holidays play a large part for many people when determining when they will embark on their pilgrimage. Many pilgrims, past and present, try to time their trip so that they arrive in Santiago de Compostela on *Dia de Santiago* (Day of Santiago), July 25th.

It is widely believed that in 1122 Pope Calixtus II gave Compostela the privilege of granting the grace of the Jubilee (this is termed a *plenary indulgence* meaning the recipient is granted a *full* pardon from any time that may have to be spent in purgatory for his/her sins) to those who visited the shrine of the Apostle St. James in the years when the saint's day, the 25th of July, fell on a Sunday. (Additional conditions of the indulgence were that while in Santiago the pilgrim would make a confession, attend Mass, give a donation for the cathedral, and perform good works.

Following the centuries-old tradition, The Holy Door, which gives access to the Cathedral from the Plaza de la Quintana, is opened on December 31st on the eve of each Holy Year, and closed off again at the end of the year.

Two weeks of cultural, religious, and political events (many of which are held on the plazas surrounding the cathedral) precede the Galician holiday of July 25th. A spectacular fireworks display is given on the Plaza de Obradoiro on the eve of July 24. And on the 25th, the Feast of St. James is held and the magnificent bota-fumeiro (the huge incense burner) is used in the cathedral.

Historically, during Holy Years the number of pilgrims soars. 2004 was the most recent Holy Year (the first of the 21st century). Throughout 2004, pilgrims flocked to Santiago from all over the world, tracing the path followed by fellow believers for centuries. That year more than 179,944 pilgrims walked or bicycled the requisite number of miles on the Camino and registered with the Pilgrim Office to receive their *Compostela* (the certificate of completion). That was three times as many as in 1999 (54,613) and double the number as in 1993 (99,436) (the two previous Holy Years).

So, whether travelers want to join the crowds or avoid them during a trip to Santiago, they should check the church's calendar to see if there will be festivities held during their planned stay. (The next Holy Years are 2010 and 2021.)

The Roncal refugio in Cizur Menor.

REGION 2

WEST NAVARRA AND LA RIOJA

Region 2 – West Navarra and La Rioja

- Pamplona to Santiago   440 miles
- Pamplona to Cizur Menor   2.8 miles
- Cizur Menor to Puente la Reina   11 miles
- Puente la Reina to Estella   13 miles
- Estella to Los Arcos   12 miles
- Los Arcos to Viana   11.5 miles
- Viana to Navarrete   13.5 miles
- Navarrete to Nájara   10 miles
- Nájara to Santa Domingo de la Calzada   12.5 miles
- Santa Domingo de la Calzada to Belorado   14 miles
- Belorado to San Juan de Ortega   15 miles

Alto de Perdón just beyond Cizur Menor.

3 • Cizur Menor to Los Arcos

Wine Flowing from Spigots?

A man hath no better thing under the sun, than to eat, and to drink, and to be merry.

—*Bible,* Ecclesiastes: 28

West of Pamplona are several ranges of hills to cross. The range between Pamplona and Puente de la Reina is windy enough to support hundreds of wind turbines generating electricity. The region is partially forested, partially agricultural. Navarra and Rioja are important wine-growing regions.

JOURNAL, DAY 5 (Wednesday, September 5): **Cizur Menor to Puente la Reina (11 miles/18 km).**

BECAUSE OF OUR fruitless attempt to get food yesterday, we again had to start our day without any breakfast. Neither the local bar or restaurant was open. Luckily, we still had some Power Bar Harvest Bars. Ralph profusely apologized for the original fuss he had made about bringing the four energy bars and I'm feeling rather smug.

After Cizur Menor, we began to leave the foothills of the Pyrenees and enter the drier and more open wine growing areas of Navarra and La Rioja. We began our climb that curves up into the hills until it reaches the Alta de Perdón Ridge, which is now lined with wind turbines.

In these hills, according to legend, a miracle occurred. A tired and thirsty pilgrim was offered water by the devil if he would disavow his faith; the pilgrim resisted. Santiago appeared and offered to lead him to water. Once at the fountain, Santiago used his own scallop shell to scoop water for the faithful pilgrim. We did, in fact, encounter a fountain that was not working, but since our water bottles were still full, we continued on without incident.

After our steep, windy climb, we reached the summit. The nearby ridges have many huge wind turbines for electricity generation. In the 1990s, the power company installed the towers and also a series of metal two-dimensional sculptures of pilgrims. Several other people were at the summit; we all had fun taking photos of each other standing alongside the dramatic, life-sized iron figures. Ralph's jacket flapping madly in the wind as he posed added to the delight of all.

We ate our olive bread, which was now several days old, but seemed even more delicious than when we purchased it on our first night. We descended on the rocky path; it was pleasant enough for hiking, but too rocky for bicycles. We went through a hamlet, still with no facilities except for a Coca Cola machine (where I was able to get my caffeine fix).

We passed fields of sunflowers along the way and I was reminded of Van Gogh's paintings of Arles. Some of the fields were full of dry sunflowers, apparently ready for harvest.

We arrived in Muruzábal about one o'clock. Several pilgrims we'd seen along the way were already enjoying the opportunity to sit in the sunshine and have lunch. We lowered ourselves into some chairs outdoors and enjoyed a lunch of bocadillos of ham and cheese, chips (I find we crave salt) and beer, which we had earned.

We continued on. The terrain became more level, then gradually descended past fields of asparagus, corn, tomatoes, and beans. We saw many tunnel-shaped, plastic-covered greenhouses and later found out that hops were grown inside. We passed under a handsome arch as we left Obanos and learned the legend of the French noblewoman, Felicia.

Murder and Remorse at Obanos

Felicia set out from the French village of Aquitaine to make the pilgrimage to Santiago de Compostela against the will of her parents and her brother, Guillermo, Duke of Aquitaine. She was so inspired by the pilgrimage that she decided to stay on in Spain as a hermit. Her brother came from France to persuade her to return and failing, killed her. Struck by remorse, Guillermo went on to Santiago. Then, he returned to Obanos to spend the rest of his life in mourning.

After his death, he was buried near the village in the *Ermita* (Hermitage) *de Nuestra Senora de Arnotegui*. His skull, now encased in silver and kept in the church of San Juan Bautista, is still used during Holy Week to bless the wine before it is given to the worshipers.

(This legend, dating from the fourteenth century, has many versions. In another one, Felicia and her brother make a pilgrimage to Compostela together and the murder takes place on the return trip when Felicia refuses to continue on to France with Guillermo.)

IT IS ALONG this section, just before crossing the medieval pilgrim bridge into Puente la Reina, that a more easterly major Camino path from Arles (in southern France) and over the central Pyrenees merges with the main trail. The area, being part of a floodplain along the river Arga, was in earlier times often difficult to cross. Numerous villages eventually were built along the way where enterprising, sometimes scheming, folk ran ferries back and forth for pilgrims en route to Santiago.

In the 11th century, a queen of Navarra, whose identity is lost to time, ordered a bridge built at the site of present day Puente la Reina—not only simplifying the crossing of the river, but also cutting the profiteering of the ferrymen. Puente la Reina is nowadays an attractive town with many sights worth a visit. I recommend that you include at least the *Iglesia de Santiago* and the *Iglesia del Crucifijo* (Church of the Crucifixion) in your stops.

The *Iglesia de Santiago*, which was established in the 1100s, was clearly well-funded. As with most of the churches along the Camino, the basic architecture, as well as the artwork within, reflect cultural changes over the course of time. The doors are Romanesque, the tower is Baroque, the southern portico is Mudejar (Islamic art created for Christians). The arch over the portico is covered with carvings of saints, sinners, and monsters, demons swallowing humans, a man fighting a lion, and so forth. Inside the church is a famous Gothic statue of Santiago Peregrino known in Basque as *Santiago Beltza* (the Black Saint).

The second church, the *Iglesia del Crucifijo*, was founded by the Knights Templar in the 12th century. Outside, you will find the porch decorated with scallop shells. Inside is the cross for which the church was named, formed in a unique "Y" shape with Christ's partially raised arms forming the arms of the Y.

The Knights Templar

The Knights Templar was an organization of warrior monks that was at the height of its power throughout Europe during the Middle Ages. Two of the original nine members of the order, Hugh de Payen (who was in the service of Charlemagne) and Andre de Montbard, went with seven companions to King Baudoin I of Jerusalem in 1118. They vowed to keep the roads and highways to Jerusalem safe—particularly for pilgrims who were easy targets for bandits and highwaymen. The knights vowed to live a life of poverty and chastity. In return the king granted them lodging and the right to an insignia, the double-barred Cross of Lorraine.

Many find it interesting that apparently the early years of the order were not spent in protecting the roads to Jerusalem, but were used to build a complex of tunnels under their lodgings on the Temple Mount. After the excavations were completed, most of the order returned to France.

As membership in the Knights Templar grew, particularly with members of the ruling families, so did its power. Donations of land and money from throughout Europe poured in; the Knights built castles in strategic places within the Holy Land and then in Europe. They acquired properties in major cities, along pilgrimage and trade routes, and in seaports as well as in the countryside. Their extensive real estate holdings, numbering in the tens of thousands, were in England, Scotland, Wales, Germany, Hungary, France, and Spain. Spain, being a Catholic country and with its Camino de Santiago, had many Knights Templar holdings. The alliance with the Knights was highly beneficial to Spain during attempts by the Moors to invade Spain.

The Knights owned many ships; they were used for both military and commercial purposes. They owned farms, mines, and vineyards. They were instrumental in planning and financially supporting the construction of numerous churches and cathedrals including, according to some scholars, the Cathedral of Chartres. They were known for their fierce and brave fighting. By the early 1200s, they had accumulated more wealth than any European kingdom. With power came autonomy. After they gained official recognition in 1128 (by the Council of Troyes), they were no longer beholden to bishops and kings, and they had to answer only to the pope. Gitlitz and Davidson state that there were 20,000 Knights Templar by the mid-1200s.

Some of the buildings, or remains of buildings, erected by the Knights Templar in Spain still exist. These include the aforementioned *Iglesia del Crucifijo* in Puente la Reina and the beautiful remains at Ponferrada, which will be discussed in Chapter 11.

Over time, certain paths to Santiago became well established. As the influence of the Knights grew, pilgrims, whether going to Rome, Jerusalem, or Santiago, finally were able to travel the routes in relative safety. The Knights were able to control large areas of the countryside. They established a banking system that aided the travelers by issuing what we today would call a debit card. Before beginning their journeys, pilgrims would establish an account with the treasurer of the local Knights Templar. After depositing the funds for the trip, they would receive a credit note in return. As the pilgrims progressed, they would hand over the chit for payment of food, lodging, alms to the church, and so forth; the merchants would note the expenses. Upon returning home, pilgrims would take the note back to the treasurer who would tally the expenses and collect or refund any balance.

Inevitably the wealth and power of the Knights aroused jealousy and anger. The French king Philip le Bell (1268–1314) hated them for two reasons. First, because as a young man, he had been refused admittance to the order, and secondly, because he later became heavily in debt to them. Sentiment turned against them, and they were suspected of acquiring their money through dishonest means. The Knights were accused of being irreligious, not believing in Christ and the Virgin Mary, and of practicing sodomy.

On Friday, October 13, 1307, Philip le Bell brought accusations against sixty of the leaders of the Knights Templar including Jacques de Molay, the Grand Master of the Order; most were held and tortured. Thousands of other knights were arrested in France. The pope dissolved the order in 1312. The Knights' holdings were confiscated and the debts owed them forgiven. The final blow to the Knights Templar came soon after. Jacques de Molay, who had been tortured in order to extract a confession (as was the case with thousands of others under the rules of the Inquisition), retracted his confession. He was sentenced to death and on March 18, 1314, was burned alive at the stake in Paris.

JOURNAL, DAY 5, resumes: Our route is now heading directly west and will continue that direction all the way to Santiago. We checked into the pleasant Hotel Jakue (a pilgrim dormitory,

Hostal Jakue, is in the basement). We thought we were due a splurge (only $50), and a conjugal night; there's little privacy in the refugios. We also enjoyed having baths and the opportunity to wash our clothes in warm water.

We received news from home via the Internet. Ralph's niece Karen and her husband are all set to leave for Russia on September 13th to pick up the little girl they are adopting. Plans for Scott and Anne's wedding are well underway; his friends are throwing a bachelor party for him. I hope I'll be trim enough after this hike to fit into the "mother of the groom" dress I've selected for his wedding. We'll be home for only two days before we have to fly to Las Vegas for the big event. Reading friends' supportive messages lifts my spirits.

JOURNAL, DAY 6 (Thursday, September 6): **Puente la Reina to Estella (13 miles/21.5 km).**

THIS WAS A long day. We're now adjusted to "Spanish time," so we awoke about six-thirty. But by the time we finished packing, and ate our pastries, juice and tea, and were out the door, it was almost nine. One of the highlights of the day came early: crossing the beautiful stone bridge of six arches on the way out of Puente la Reina.

We next came to Cirauqui. One moment we were hiking along in what seemed like the middle of nowhere; then suddenly the ancient restored hilltop village came into view. The unobstructed views from the village obviously made it a strategic location for defending the surrounding area. The name, Cirauqui (in Basque, *"nest of vipers"*), dates from the ninth century. Nowadays, there are a few places to obtain food, but no lodging.

We were quickly through the small town. Those who stop long enough to enjoy it (which unfortunately we did not) will see many old mansions still bearing their original coats-of-arms. The *Iglesia de San Roman* has a Mudejar-style arch similar to the one at Puente la Reina. The church's interior has several beautiful *retablos* (a series of carvings behind the main altar).

Although much of the Camino follows the route of the ancient Roman roads, the section between Cirauqui and Lorca has the best-preserved stretch of the original Roman paving stones. About a mile and a half after Cirauqui, the trail crosses a small Gothic bridge (with the characteristic pointed arches). Soon after, we passed the hilltop ruins of the town of Urbe (which flourished from the 11th to the 18th century). A similar bridge, a little farther on, spans the *Rio Salado*, once known as the *River of Death*.

The Legend of the River of Death
—adapted from the *Codex Calixtinus*, translated by Melczer

It was the custom of the inhabitants of the village near the Rio Salado to sit by that stream, sharpening their knives. When pilgrims approached and asked, "Is this good water?," the villagers would assure them that it was. When the travelers let their horses drink, the animals immediately fell down dead. The villagers would skin the horses with their knives, and keep the meat and hides.

JOURNAL, DAY 6, resumes: Because it was September and nearing harvest time, the grapes were heavy on the vines. We were intrigued by the fact that some vines had both red and white grapes. We walked past many miles of grapes, tasted a few—absolutely wonderful—a warm burst of juicy sweetness!

We stopped in Lorca at the town's central fountain. Our feet get very hot and sweaty and that adds to my blister problem. And so it was heavenly to be able to fill our new collapsible plastic basin with water and have a footbath.

At lunchtime, as frequently occurs, the proprietor gave us our choices verbally. And, as usual, we couldn't understand so we asked her to write them. She was very sweet; she brought out a small plate and spooned out a sample of each item of the first course: garbanzo beans, green beans, and macaroni. The beans were a welcome treat. Up until now *verduras* has been a plate of peas (which I hate). A pitcher of wine was delivered.

Then came the main course of meatballs with gravy, followed by flan for dessert, and tea. Our tab was $14.50 (including the wine). We've found that additional *Vino de Mesa* (table wine) is very inexpensive (usually about four dollars a bottle) and good.

This is a prime agriculture area: in addition to the grapes, we saw a lot of asparagus—mostly kept from direct sunlight and later canned—fig trees, tomatoes, and beans. It was interesting to note that though we were often near food crops, we hadn't seen pilgrims picking fruit along the way. Obviously the thousands who pass by here yearly could rip off a lot, but I presumed that they feel, as we do, that it's not ours to pick. (I hasten to add that what we'd tasted was from a bunch of grapes that had been recently dropped by someone else.) There are also huge mounds of wild blackberries, but they tend to be small and rather tasteless.

We've noticed that, as we approach villages, the tallest structure in town was most often the church. (Later, on the plains of the *meseta*, we would see the church spires long before we would see the town.)

So far, most of our Camino path has been on trails and away from roadways. Its condition and composition varies much as park trails anywhere: tramped dirt, gravel, or stones. It's sometimes littered with sheep droppings or cow pies. We much prefer the sections where we follow ancient Roman roads or old dirt lanes through pastures to the portions that some local government has paved in the name of improvement. Not only is the pavement less interesting and historic, it's also much harder on our feet. However, when we enter small towns and large cities, we're generally on sidewalks or streets.

JOURNAL RESUMES: WE walked on, using our umbrellas for relief from the intense heat. When we reached Estella, we found that the refugio was full. The hosts referred us on to the local youth-hostel, which, luckily, was very clean, and did not take us off the route. We knew that since youth-hostels allow most any traveler to stay, not just pilgrims with credentials, the rules might be different from those of the refugios. We investigated and found out that curfew was midnight and then set out for dinner, happy that we didn't need to hurry home afterwards. We had *tapas* of omelets filled with cheese, zucchini, and ham.

It came as somewhat of a surprise to return to the hostel and find all the room lights already off even though it wasn't yet nine. We couldn't read or write and had to set up our bedding and get ready for bed with our flashlights. Then, even with a sleeping pill, I couldn't get to sleep for a long time because of the pain in my right calf. (It is an on-going problem, pre-dating the trip, but it seems to be compounded by overuse.). Once I did fall asleep, I slept soundly.

JOURNAL, DAY 7 (Friday, September 7): **Estella to Los Arcos (12 miles/19 km).**

TODAY WE HAD a tasty *desayuno* (breakfast) of custard pastries and hot tea. We set out feeling well-rested and fed; we were eagerly anticipating an early morning stop at a local winery, the Bodegas Irache. We had read that the bodega had a wine fountain where pilgrims could get a cup of free wine. We had carefully saved the plastic cups from our room at the hotel back in Puente de la Reina.

We arrived early, about nine. We found the spigots, labeled *tinto* and *blanco* (red and white). We paused to read the inscription: "Peregrino, if you want to reach Santiago with strength and vitality, have a drink of this great wine and toast to happiness." We lifted the spigots. Nothing. Then we read that they are not turned on until ten-thirty and then only for a few hours each day. I was really disappointed, but we filled our cups with water and continued on. (I've since read that Bodegas Irache's Fuente de Vino (wine fountain) gives out approximately 35,000 liters of wine a year to pilgrims.)

The Wine Growing Regions of Spain

—David Andrew)

Tapas and vino—could it get any better? Tapa bars are gaining in popularity across the U.S. and rightly so—diners can order several small plates of delicious appetizers—and not be limited to one entree. What better to pair them with than a glass of Spanish wine?

Spain is the largest grape-growing country in the world. Wine has been made here for 3,000 years, so there's no shortage of tradition and history to draw on. But innovation and modernization have breathed new life into this country's wines. In fact, exports of Spanish wine to the U.S. have risen 62 percent over the past [several] years, so the world is clearly rediscovering Spain's vinous treasures.

The indigenous grape variety responsible for Spain's highest quality red wines is Tempranillo, which marries well with the American oak traditionally used to mature it. But the more familiar Cabernet Sauvignon and Merlot are gaining ground and adding yet more diversity to the country's wide range of wines.

Quality Spanish wine is classified by region of origin, *Denominacion de Origen (DO)* of which there are more than 50. Each DO has its own *Consejo Reguladro,* which regulate the growing, making and marketing of its region's wines and ensures compliance with regional standards, much like the French Appellation Control system. Spain has one higher-quality classification, *Denominacion de Origen Califacada (DOC)*, and to date only one region has been awarded this status: Rioja.

Spain's premier-quality wine-growing region, and perhaps its most famous, Rioja produces mostly red wines in the north of the country. Typically a blend of Tempranillo, Garnacha, Mazuela and Graciano, these wines have all the richness and style of a matador's cape.

Riojas are labeled according to the length of oak maturation they have received, and this is often a good indication of quality, too. Crianza means that the wine has spent one year in oak.

Reserva must spend three years in the cellar, including a minimum of one year in oak and one year in bottle. Gran Reserva, made only in the best vintages, must spend at least two years in oak and three in bottle before release, resulting in wines that are smooth, silky, and sensuous.

Navarra, a neighboring region to the east, makes wines in a similar style, but historically used more of the Garnacha grape (the same as Grenache in France). Today the region's most exciting wines are single-varietal Tempranillos, Cabernet Sauvignons, Merlots and blends of the three. International grape varieties take on a distinctly Spanish flair here.

South of Rioja and Navarra is Ribera del Duero, home to Spain's most celebrated (and expensive) wine: Vega Sicilia. The predominant grape here is a local strain of the Tempranillo, although Vega Sicilia is 35 percent Cabernet Sauvignon. Pesquera, a wine that nips at the heels of Vega Sicilia in quality at a fraction of the price, uses only Tempranillo in its dense, concentrated, complex wine designed for the long haul.

But it's not all red. Among the best whites is the bright, fresh, floral and fragrant wine made from the Albarino grape in the Rias Basixas region of Galicia. And then, of course, there's Cava, Spain's sparkling wine. Made using the champagne method, Cava can provide a real alternative to champagne and offers incredible value at the same time.

It's impossible to talk about Spanish wine without paying homage to Spain's unique and wonderful sherry (Jerez in Spanish). The Jerez region, around the town of Jerez de la Frontera, is situated in the country's extreme south. The soil is composed mainly of dazzling white chalk, creating a bizarre but beautiful landscape.

There are three main types of sherry: Fino, Amontillado and Oloroso. Fino is bone dry, should be served chilled and is wonderfully refreshing. It is drunk as an aperitif but is also perfect with olives, tapas and fish. Oloroso is rich and full in flavor, it can be dry or sweet, but the best will always be complex with the aroma of dried fruit and nuts. Salud!

JOURNAL, DAY 7, resumes: Trails today were pretty comfortable walking, mostly of gravel or dirt. We're very impressed by the with the well-maintained farms with their row upon row of well-tended plants. We love walking by the vineyards: their knobby vines, restful-looking green leaves, huge purple clusters of grapes contrasting with the deep-red clay soil.

We passed a Moorish structure, an old water-storage building with one side open revealing wide steps going down to the water within. Before this trip, I'd never considered how many different cultures have either lived in or invaded this country, and we are now seeing that diversity reflected in the architecture as well as in the layout and placement of cities and towns.

We passed through the tiny village of Villamayor de Monjardín. The hamlet is perched on a hillside with magnificent views of the surrounding countryside. Its backdrop is the mountain peak, Monjardín, and the ruins of *Castillo de San Esteban* (St. Stephen's Castle). I wanted to stay; it was one of those charming settings where one can easily imagine renting a garret and spending a year writing or painting.

We next came to Los Arcos, a town inhabited since Roman times. Its location on the Odron River, in a land of fertile soil, with a nearby hillside castle for protection, was optimal for settlement. From medieval times until relatively recently, Los Arcos was a rich market center offering everything from produce to money-changing. In Los Arcos is the *Iglesia de Santa María de la Asuncion*. If you are able to attend the pilgrims' mass, or otherwise visit the interior, you will find a 17th-century retablo of the Baroque style that is considered one of the finest on the Camino.

Though the terrain was good, the miles still tire. I start out the days feeling pretty good, but as the hours and miles add up, my feet begin to hurt more and more. By the end of the day, my feet feel like blocks of wood and I am practically hobbling the last few miles. I don't mind being tired, but the pain is discouraging.

Again the refugio was full, and the host who ran it was clearly upset about it. "Yesterday," he said, "we opened at noon and we were full by one. It's not fair to you because you're honest. Others take the bus and get here first. We throw them out when we can, but we can't catch them all," he continued.

But the private refuge he referred us to is fine: only six beds in our room and more beds upstairs. The owner brought me an ice pack when I asked for something cold to hold against my sore leg. It's breezy here, and the laundry we put out a couple of hours ago is already dry.

I've become more comfortable with the refugios. Ever since our initial confusing and anxiety-provoking stay at Roncesvalles, each night has seemed easier, but we still worry about not finding a place to stay.

Usually the beds are reasonably comfortable, and I can find a lower bunk. However, I still usually wake up in a sweat because my sleeping bag is warm and the other people prefer to close the windows at night. I'm used to a colder sleeping room.

In general people are very considerate, keep the places clean, and are quiet after closing. Few snore. There is the early morning hubbub; it's stressful for a couple of reasons. First of all, it cuts our rest time. Secondly, we know that they are getting a jump on the upcoming night's scarce beds. We've talked about joining the early morning race, but we've decided not to because it isn't light when many of them set out. We didn't come here to walk across the country in the dark, and, as I said before, you can't see the trail markers.

I've had some thoughts on what travelers of the Camino have called visions or passions or revelations. Not to be cynical, but I wonder how many of these experiences are caused by heat, exhaustion, or lack of food or water.

I also am reflecting on the interesting rules of sanitation and cleanliness. In some ways, I think the United States scores higher; in other ways, Spain does. The houses are beautifully kept, at least judging from the exterior. Window boxes brimming with flowers and wrought iron balconies adorned with potted plants are signs of pride. The large, outdoor gardens are neatly done. Sidewalks are often of elaborate stonework or patterns.

What I don't like, however, is the litter. In the bars, for example, people sitting at the counters drop used napkins, empty sugar packets, toothpicks, and such at their feet. And, of course, the toilet paper littering the trailside is gross, but on the other hand, the bathrooms in bars and restaurants are usually spotless. In addition, the stoops, sidewalks, and streets are usually swept or washed clean, even though the constant wind in some areas surely makes it difficult to keep them litter-free. (I wish the otherwise-beautiful city of San Francisco would take note.)

JOURNAL, DAY 7, resumes: During today's hike, I told Ralph that this was a decision day: that I was fed up with pain. But, as it turned out, my feet feel better tonight. I think it's because I changed to thinner socks and loosened my laces; now my feet have more room.

We are starting to see the same people time and again; that's fun. We have three women in our room tonight who speak English: two from Germany and Pamela from England. We had an exceptionally pleasant dinner because of our companions, the German women, Marguerita and Leis. We've been starved for conversation, so because Marguerita spoke fair English, and Leis a bit, we enjoyed sharing a meal with them.

Marguerita gestured towards the bottle of wine when the waiter delivered it. "We could have had two bottles of wine, one for each set of us, if we had waited to join you at your table," she laughed. Marguerita shared her joke with her friends, and although the fixed-price dinner usually includes a full bottle of wine, none of us felt deprived about sharing the bottle with three others, rather than one.

Ralph and I had trout again, for probably the third time. I've actually learned how to de-bone it at my advanced age. I had the *mixta* (mixed salad), which is usually served topped with tuna. Ralph had green beans. We both had rice pudding; we are really overdoing on flan and rice pudding, I'm afraid.

Anna, who has been helpful along the way, is here with us again. I asked her about the medical care that is sometimes offered at the refugios. She said that Spanish citizens have a card for free care, but she felt certain that a doctor would treat us free of charge also. If only the U.S. were as enlightened!

We think that we've been lucky with the weather we've encountered. Because it is fall, most of the fields are now stubble. In this land of subtle shades of gold, tan, and brown, the dark, charred fields that remain after the burning off after the fall harvest are a visual treat.

Spanish Olives

Shelly Keller writes in *Solano Magazine*, "Olive oil has been around for at least 3,500 years and the olive tree has symbolized longevity, fertility, maturity and peace in many cultures. The Bible includes an estimated 140 references to olive oil, which has been used through the ages as a lamp fuel, medicine, hair and skin tonic, a balm to anoint sovereigns and priests, and even as a weapon (when it was boiled and thrown over castle walls onto attackers)." She continues, "Research has linked olive oil to the prevention of breast and prostate cancer, diabetes, hypertension, and rheumatoid arthritis."

The olive trees of Spain (like the Spanish vineyards) enjoy a long history. These handsome trees grow slowly and usually live to an old age. Olives are picked in the winter and then are used for olive oil or brined to eat as tapas. Ninety-two percent of Spain's olives are used for their healthful oil. Olive oil not only tastes good, it appears to be superior to other oils in our diet. Olives are low in cholesterol, and have many beneficial dietary benefits.

Spain's olive oil is divided into four classes: Virgin Olive oil,

Refined Olive oil, Olive oil, and Pomace Olive oil. Within the Virgin Olive oil class, there are three levels of quality (in descending order): extra, average, and strong.

Extra Virgin oil is defined by the International Oil Council as having the following attributes: produced solely using mechanical means, produced without solvents or refining processes, produced at a temperature of 81 degrees Fahrenheit or less, an oleic acid content of less than one percent; no "defects" as judged by an authorized tasting panel. It is made from the first cold-pressing of the olives. Ideally, consumers will use young, extra virgin olive oil for everything from salads to frying. With the reasonable prices of the Spanish oil, there is no need to save extra virgin oils for special occasions.

Refined Olive oil takes virgin oil with unpleasant tastes or high acidity and refines it to make it tasty. It's acceptable for consumption, but lacks the Virgin oil's characteristic taste.

Olive Oil is a combination of Refined Oil and Virgin Oil, therefore falling between the two previous categories in taste. It is mild in taste and golden in color.

Pomace Oil is made by refining the olive oil pressing. It has little flavor and is primarily used for fried foods.

Professional tasters test the oil in a room free of other scents. They sample it much like wine tasters—with the exception of looking at the color—the olive oil should be in a colored glass so that the color of the olive oil does not influence their evaluation. They smell, swirl, then sip the oil. Excellent oils will taste like olive juice: with fruitiness, some bitterness, and pungency.

The main varietal, arbequina, is considered by most to be Spain's premier olive and is grown primarily in the Catalonia area. It produces an extra virgin oil with an intense fresh-oil flavor. Backed by Spanish investors, Arbequina is increasingly planted in California—particularly in the northern California Oroville area which has long been known as the 'Olive Capital of California'—but has primarily been planted with Mission olives for canning and Italian varietals for oil.

Leaving Obanos.

Church spire on the horizon.

4 • Los Arcos to Nájera

Festival in Viana

Keep your face to the sunshine and you cannot see the shadow.

—Helen Keller

JOURNAL, DAY 8 *(Saturday, September 8):* **Los Arcos to Viana (11.5 miles/18.5 km).**

WE HAD BREAKFAST at the refugio. For a minimal fee, about $1.75, we had a few tiny grapes (when I think of the delicious ones that are growing in the countryside!) and a small, juicy apple from our host's garden. Hard, square biscuits, with tasty homemade marmalade and peach jam accompanied the fruit. We started hiking at eight with stops for tea, and later for lunch, which was our usual sandwich on a roll, soda, and fruit enjoyed picnic style.

Most of the fields we passed today were bare; the growing season is over, I suppose. Some grapes still around. The soil is now almost gray; we've left the red soils of the foothills. We are undoubtedly behind where we *should* be, but hope to be able to make up the miles later. The soreness of my legs continues to plague me most nights, but taking Ibuprofen last night allowed me to sleep well. Or maybe after one night of being awake, I'm so tired I have to sleep the next!

Today's hike was less exciting visually than it has been the last few days, but I am beginning to find my pace. I actually felt good all day. And even though it's becoming hotter, our umbrellas work wonderfully to shade us from the sun. It's also better when we stop relatively early in the day since the heat really builds in the mid-afternoon.

We arrived here in Viana about two-thirty. The whole town is in party mode; it's their feast day. The streets and the central plaza are filled with crowds. Propped up in front of the church are three *gigantes* (giants) brought out for special occasions.

IN HER BOOK *Festivals of Western Europe*, Dorothy Gladys Spicer describes *gigantes* and *cabezudos:* "*Gigantes*—some of them twenty to thirty feet tall—are walking cardboard and canvas figures, concealing men who dance and perform to the traditional music of the gralla, or flute, and tamboril, or small drum. The giants often represent Spanish kings and queens, or famous literary and historical figures."

Though we didn't see any in Viana, traditionally the giant figures are joined by dwarf ones, *Cabezudos*. Spicer explains, "The cabezudos, on the other hand, are grotesque dwarfs with immense heads. These puppets caricature different professions or personalities," writes Spicer.

JOURNAL, DAY 8 resumes: A temporary bullfight ring has been set up, and we've heard there will be a running of the bulls in the morning; that surprises me because it will be a Sunday and I assumed that it would be a day of church going and rest. There are bicyclists madly racing around too. We've noticed that one channel on the TV is always broadcasting bicycle races in one place or another. Racing is a big deal here.

The refugios are crowded, but we have not had to sleep on the floor yet. Today's refugio has five rooms, each with an average of nine beds. Ralph's had to take the top one of a three-high set of bunk beds. I have a middle bunk in a different room. No pillows, but I can use my jacket or something. The bathroom on our floor has two showers and one toilet, so we had to wait a while and then found the room as steamy as a sauna.

I'm sitting in the dining room. It's large and contains a long table for writing or reading. One wall has stove and sink for those who want to prepare their own food. There's also a laundry room with a couple of washtubs and an indoor drying area with racks and lines. Considering the humidity level brought about by all of the wet clothing hanging, we'll be very lucky if anything dries.

Viana is known for more than its beauty. It is also known for its connection with the infamous Cesare Borgia. Cesare, an Italian warlord usually thought of in terms of murder and mayhem he caused in his native country, was also an adventurer in Spain. In 1506, he lost a battle there and was imprisoned. He escaped to Navarra where, in a story of political intrigue, he joined forces with the King of Navarra to protect Viana from a siege by Count Louis de Beaumont. Cesare rode out alone to launch a surprise attack on Beaumont's rear guard. He died of some two dozen wounds and was subsequently buried as a hero in the *Iglesia de Santa María,* the church on the town square.

JOURNAL, DAY 9 (Sunday, September 9): **Viana to Navarrete (13.5 miles/22.5 km).**

LAST NIGHT IN Viana was a lot of fun. When we went out to watch the festivities in the town square (*Plaza de la Fueros*), we were invited to join the parade. Soon we were caught up in the procession as the band, the *Gigantes,* and the other celebrants wound through the neighboring streets like serpents through a rocky field.

Everyone else appeared to be shepherding their children, but they didn't kick us out. Afterwards, we sat in the town square while various bands played everything from Benny Goodman to romantic Spanish ballads. I could not help but be struck by the fact that it was eight in the evening and that people of all ages were coming and going and the kids were free to run around (as kids should be free to do!).

We went to dinner and then returned to the refugio where we fell into bed exhausted. Luckily for the pilgrims who celebrated late into the night, the refugio did not lock up tight at ten o'clock, but allowed people to prop the door open and stay out late. The fiesta is scheduled to run for three more days.

We set out this morning before the scheduled running of the bulls. We are still operating under the pressure of having to move along to find a place to sleep at night. But, though we were sorry to miss that colorful event, we did have an exciting start to the day.

When we walked out of the refugio at seven-thirty, a band was already moving through the streets. One of the young men grabbed my hands, and pulled me into the parade. Loaded down as I was with my backpack, I couldn't do more than a few springy dance steps, so I quickly dropped out. We watched as they continued up the street.

When we left Viana, the lighting was particularly dramatic: dark-blue clouds pasted on a light-blue sky. We looked back one last time to see the magnificent, ancient high walls that still surround much of the town—a memorable, lovely place.

Bullfighting

Though many in Spain oppose bullfighting, it is as popular as ever. To many, it is such an important part of their heritage that opposing it comes as a threat to their culture. Nowadays, bulls are bred and well cared for in the years before their few minutes of fame. Before heading for the bullring, the bull must be a minimum of four years old.

The bullfight consists of three parts: *tercio de varas, tercio de banderillas,* and *tercio de muleta.* In the first part, *tercio de varas,* the *matador* uses his (or her) red cape, *capa,* to goad the bull. The *picadores* (horsemen with lances), with the assistance of their *peones* (helpers), thrust the steel-pointed lances into the shoulders of the bull, attempting to weaken it. In the second stage, the banderilleros (who, are on foot) attempt to thrust pairs of *banderillas* (barbed darts) along the bull's spine. And in *tercio de muleta* the matador again makes passes with the capa to provoke the injured bull. At the climax, the matador thrusts the sword and kills the bull. Sometimes, when the bull has shown great courage, the crowd will wave white handkerchiefs—asking that the bull be spared.

Though there are hundreds of sites for bullfighting: some permanent, others temporary. The following are Spain's most popular:

* Madrid's beautiful Plaza de Toros de Las Ventas holds bullfights, *corridas,* every Sunday during the season from May to October, and daily during May's fiesta of San Isidro.

* Ronda, a city in southern Spain dating back to Moorish times, has the Plaza de Toros, "The Spiritual Home of Bullfighting." For a matador, fighting at Plaza de Toros (inaugurated in 1785), is comparable to a singer appearing on stage at Carnegie Hall. Pedro Romero (b. 1754) is considered the father of modern bullfighting, and is attributed with killing over 6,000 bulls during his career.

* In Seville is the Plaza de Toros de la Maestranza, which was constructed between 1761 and 1881. This magnificent bullring, which is faced in the Baroque style, holds 14,000 fans. On the west side is a gate, *Puerta de Principle* (Prince's Gate), through which revelers carry triumphant matadors. The season here begins on Easter; guided tours are led year-round.

JOURNAL, DAY 9, resumes: Another intriguing thing we saw today, in an industrial area just before we entered Logroño, were several crosses—fashioned with scraps of wood—inserted into a chain-link fence. (My mother later told me that the Basque sheepherders used to do this in the vicinity of her father's sheep ranch in northeastern Oregon.) The vineyards continue, but the countryside is more level now.

Our hike today took us through the major city of Logroño, and even though it was a Sunday, much was open. This is in stark contrast to the small villages where we're lucky if we find anything open. After we had lunch, I was very happy to find a cyber-café where I could once again get on the Internet. I sent a message to a friend asking her to save a copy of all my e-mails. Even though I am only writing a few pages a day in a journal, I think I could write a book.

The clouds we saw early morning had long since vanished. It was a comfortable day in the 60s–70s. On the outskirts of Logroño, we walked through *Pantano de la Grajera*. It's a huge regional park that was created when the Rio Iregua was dammed in the late 1880s. The local fishermen now enjoy the reservoir that was formed. It was a scene much like home: men setting up to barbecue, and picnic tables covered with bags of food and coolers filled with beverages.

Walkers out for an afternoon constitutional shared the wide trail with young children, wobbling on their first bicycle rides while steadied by parents running alongside. Unlike our regional trails, there were no joggers (in fact we have yet to see a jogger). And instead of the sweatshirts and sweatpants we're more likely to see back home, people here were dressed in street clothes: the women wearing skirts, the men in slacks and shirts.

DESPITE OUR REASONABLE start before eight, by the time we arrived here in Navarrete, there was only room if we were willing to sleep on the floor. The nearby hostel was also full. Of course it was very discouraging to walk all day and then find the refugios full. It turns what would otherwise be a peaceful experience into a race with the pressure to beat someone else out of a place. I'm finding myself resentful of those who leave so early in the morning and suspicious of those who get to the evening's place early. We've decided to do a shorter hop tomorrow in hopes we'll get to our destination earlier. We can never beat the bicyclists, but their options are somewhat limited, too, since many places either won't house them or won't take them in until a later hour.

We continued on to the outskirts of town and found a new, upscale hotel. So, it turned out well for us. The rate is sixty dollars (which is inexpensive for a hotel of this quality back home). That is affordable for us, but we've talked to people who are going to have to shorten their trip because they can't afford to be continually forced to pay the hotel rates.

Dinner started with the area's typical iceberg lettuce salad, but the pork was flattened and "chicken fried," and quite wonderful. And I am looking forward to my own bed, as my leg pain kept me awake again last night.

The area around Navarrete is well-known for its wine and mushroom-growing. Both are kept in the numerous dark, cool *bodegas* (caves) of the surrounding hills. Though the town is relatively small, population 2,000, it has several points of interest.

The first is the *Iglesia de la Asuncion* in town's center; it has one of Spain's finest retablos. Next, on the outskirts of town as you leave, is the 19th century cemetery. Its magnificent Romanesque entrance dates from the 13th century; its carvings depict dramatic, historic battles (such as the one between Roland and Ferragut described on pg. 71) and everyday scenes of pilgrim life. The cemetery's entrance was moved to its present site from the former pilgrim hospital of St. John at Acre. And lastly, there is a plaque dedicated to Alice de Craer, a pilgrim who was killed in an accident in 1986 while cycling to Santiago.

JOURNAL, DAY 10 (Monday, September 10): **Navarrete to Nájera (10 miles/16 km).**

IT WAS SUCH a treat to sleep last night in a real bed; for once I did not wake up in a cold sweat. We had breakfast in the hotel too. Somehow, I ended up with toast (boring!) instead of a croissant, but the compensation was freshly-squeezed orange juice. The juicer is fascinating; it has a mechanism that automatically rolls the oranges down into the machine.

The penalty for a leisurely breakfast was a late start—almost nine—but our walk was shorter than usual and quite pleasant. Nothing hurt (much), and it wasn't too hot. It's finally registered with us that many of the stop signs we've seen are in English. We're told that this is a carryover from World War II that migrated south.

The vineyards continue to be the main crop; plowed fields are interspersed. We are continuing to walk west with mountain ranges far to the north and south of us.

The most fun today was coming upon the "rock way." For a stretch of almost 300 yards, there were stone cairns—small stacks of rocks—along the trail. (We'd call them *ducks* in the Sierra.) There were hundreds of these little statues, none more than a foot high. I added a few rocks to some, all the while wondering who began this "art work," and when.

We were later to see other places along the trail where there were more accumulations—most often at some point of accomplishment: the top of a long hill, or the end of a long dry stretch, so we decided that they were stones of celebration. When Sue Kenney narrates her experiences of the Camino on her CD, *Stone by Stone*, she says that these are "worry stones." Each time you place a stone, some of your worry goes with it, and by the time you get to Santiago, most of your worries will be gone. She adds that you can also place stones for others' worries.

I prefer my interpretation. I enjoyed these little bits of whimsy. It meant a lot when I was trudging along to be reminded that many others have traveled this path and I was not alone.

THE ENVIRONS OF Nájera the scene of a legendary battle between the forces of France's Charlemagne and the Turks. The Turks had with them a giant, alledgedly "seven meters high," known as Ferragut. Ferragut had fought, and slain, two dozen opponents, one at a time. Roland rose to the challenge. They fought off and on for three days; during one of the quiet times, "Ferragut let slip that his only vulnerable point was his navel. At last the two agreed to fight a final time, with the winner to be whichever of them professed the true religion. Ferragut fell on Roland, thinking to crush him with his weight, but the French hero stuck him with his dagger—guess where? When Ferragut died, Roland successfully captured Nájera and released the Christian prisoners." (Gitlitz and Davidson, pg. 136)

JOURNAL, DAY 10, resumes: The refugio here in Nájera is in an old monastery. The monastery itself was originally built into the red cliffs that define the northern edge of the city, and the interior of the monastery has caves within the cliff. The twelve- to fourteen-inch beams that support the roof are hand-hewn and probably date from when this monastery was built in the 15th or 16th century. Certainly we do not see trees of that diameter in the forests now.

The city is fairly large, but we raced, literally, through the new section to get to this older section so we would have a place at the refugio. When we arrived at one-fifteen, the refuge was not yet open, but there were already dozens of backpacks lined up at the door, and people were milling about. Even so, we were relatively near the front of the line. We did, however, get beds, and wonder of wonders, they were given out in an organized manner. We were assigned a numbered bed, thereby avoiding the usual free-for-all.

When I plopped down on the beds I discovered that the beds are constructed with a metal bar that runs the length of the bed down the middle, with wooden slats going sideways to support the mattress. Unfortunately, I can feel the metal bar, so it will be a challenge to get comfortable.

Late in the day, our friend, Paula, and another woman she is currently walking with, arrived. The beds were all taken, so they had to sleep on the floor with only their thin foam mats. A man offered Paula's companion his bed. She said, "No." Then he pulled his mattress off his bed and dragged it over for her.

When she refused again, he looked very disappointed. I think people try very hard to be kind; many times I've seen them collect extra mats for those without them.

There was an informal potluck going on. People were preparing what they had brought, and then combining the results. They offered it to others, but we had already eaten, so couldn't join them.

We stayed in Nájera at the *Monasterio de Santa María de Real*, which surrounds the cave where the monastery originated. According to legend, in 1044, the Navarran King Garcia III was hunting for partridges and saw his hawk chase one of the birds into a cave. The king followed and came upon a statue of the Virgin Mary, with a vase of lilies, a lit lamp, and a bell nearby. The hawk and partridge were sitting peaceably side by side. Upon seeing this miracle, he decided to build a chapel in honor of Mary. Nowadays visitors may view a replica of the statue of the Virgin Mary and a vase of lilies, as well as the tombs containing the remains of Garcia III and many other members of the Navarran royalty.

Waiting for the Nájera refugio to open.

5 • Nájera to Santo Domingo de la Calzada

The Legend of the Chickens of Santo Domingo de la Calzada

There is a certain relief in change, even though it be from bad to worse; as I have found in travelling in a stagecoach that it is often a comfort to shift one's position and be bruised in a new place.
—Washington Irving (*Wolfert's Roost*, "Creole Village")

***JOURNAL, DAY 11 (Tuesday, September 11):* Nájera to Santo Domingo de la Calzada (12.5 miles/20.5 km)**

WE HAD AN early start today. As I've said before, people start jumping out of bed before light, at six o'clock or so. They try to be quiet, but when thirty people are trying to be quiet, yet are packing things in plastic bags, zipping zippers, and flashlight beams are bouncing around, sleep is impossible. So, though I slept little last night, I decided it was a lost cause and woke Ralph. We were out by six-forty.

It was indeed dark! We couldn't see the way to go, or the arrows, in the dark. We followed some other hikers, and had no problems, but agreed it just wasn't safe. It really wasn't light enough to see until seven-fifteen, and sunrise wasn't until almost eight.

However, we discovered another advantage to starting early:

we beat the heat. It was hotter today than yesterday, but our umbrellas were helpful. Using them keeps us cooler than a hat would and sometimes we even can trap a pleasant breeze. (For several years we have been using umbrellas to ward off the sun on backpacking trips—a method we learned from the ultralight backpacking "guru," Ray Jardine.)

Today we progressed through a long, long plain with mountain ranges on either side far in the distance. We're still seeing some vineyards, but we're beginning to see different crops. We stopped for a moment to watch workers harvesting potatoes. Perhaps it's a romantic notion, but I was pleased to see that the work was still being done using manual labor; I suppose in a few years it will all be mechanized. We saw a lone sheepherder with his dogs and flock; we hadn't seen any others for days. We passed through two small villages.

WHEN WE ARRIVED at our refugio in Santo Domingo de la Calzada, we were greeted, and escorted into the sleeping-room. I thought I had died and gone to heaven. (It's interesting how one's perspective changes with deprivation!) Though the room was as large as a gymnasium, and about as glamorous, its two rows of beds neatly lined up against the walls was a welcome sight. And there were no bunk beds.

Gradually the twenty-eight beds became occupied, and the last five arrivals had to pull out the spare mattresses and sleep on the floor, but still there was ample space for all. There were separate men's and women's restrooms with four showers in each. Amazingly, the water was hot. There were also lots of wash tubs and outdoor clotheslines. The kitchen was in a separate building. The accommodations were among the best we've found yet.

Santo Domingo de la Calzada's cathedral also has a retablo of note. Its backdrop—of the type used in a theater— is of the style used during mass since Gothic times. We enjoyed learning the history of Santo Domingo, the saint who established the cathedral of this city, and the story of the chickens who live in an honored niche inside the church.

It's hard to imagine it nowadays, but a thousand years ago this region was one of the more dangerous sections of the pilgrimage. The area near Santo Domingo de la Calzada was swampy and forested; the area just ahead, Montes de Oca, was steep and hilly. Bandits and wild animals thrived; travelers feared for their lives.

This began to change for the better in the 11th century when a local shepherd, Domingo Garcia, decided to become a monk. He studied at two monasteries, but failed at his studies. Nevertheless, he was determined to spend his life in religious service; he began by helping Cardinal San Gregorio Ostiense to improve travel conditions in Rioja.

He returned to his home in Oja and became a hermit living near the Oja River. Desiring to dedicate his life to helping pilgrims, he first set out to build a stone bridge across the river. Then he began working to clear a trail through the area. A local legend goes that he was aided in this endeavor by angels who continued to cut the trees whenever Domingo stopped to pray. In time, Domingo was joined by Juan Velazquez who became his disciple and helped him construct bridges at Logroño, Santo Domingo de la Calzada, and Nájera.

In the mid-11th century, King Garcia III (of Nájera) gave Domingo permission to use an old fort as a pilgrim hospice. Domingo lived to about 90; his last years were devoted to building a church in the town that had sprung up around his hospice. His body was buried in the original church; his tomb can be viewed in the present-day cathedral in a crypt under the main floor.

THE CATHEDRAL IS worthy of a lengthy visit; there is art of many periods with hundreds of carved or painted figures in scenes depicting various religious stories and motifs as well as the life of Santo Domingo. Without a doubt, the chickens in a coop just inside the cathedral's west entrance will fascinate even the most footsore traveler.

The Chickens of Santo Domingo de la Calzada

A father, mother and their handsome son were on pilgrimage from their home in Germany to Santiago and stopped at an inn in the village of Santo Domingo de la Calzada. The innkeeper's daughter attempted to seduce the son. When he refused her advances, she crept into his room and hid some silver in his belongings.

The next morning she accused him of theft. He was hauled before the town magistrate, protesting his innocence, but it did no good. He was promptly hanged—as was the custom of the time—and left on the gibbet as a warning to others. The grieving parents continued their pilgrimage to Santiago.

Upon their return, they stopped by Santo Domingo to pay their respects to their son. When they approached the gallows, to their astonishment they found that their son was still hanging, but was alive and smiling. He greeted them warmly and told them that St. James had been supporting his feet. The parents rushed to the mayor to get the son cut down. The mayor, in the midst of eating his chicken dinner, refused to do it, and said, "Your son could not be alive, any more than these chickens could fly from this plate." At that moment the chickens flew from his plate, so everyone rushed to the gallows and cut down the son; the major gave him a full pardon.

(There is more than one version of this legend. Some versions have the young man's feet held up by Santo Domingo, some by St. James.)

Ever since that day, two chickens, which are rotated frequently, have been kept in a cage in the church to encourage pilgrims. Nowadays the pilgrims feed them for luck: it's said that if the chickens crow when you see them on pilgrimage, it is considered good luck. They crowed for us!

Many people believe in the miracle of the chickens at Santo Domingo, others have their doubts. This was as true in earlier times as in modern times. A contemporary pilgrim, Rosina Lila, was somewhat skeptical. When she visited the cathedral in 2004, she asked one of the priests for his interpretation of the legend and forwarded this account:

"I went to the pilgrims' mass at the Cathedral at eight o'clock. The officiating priests invite pilgrims to remain, after Mass, if they wish, for an explanation of the meaning of the imagery and the history of the church. A multilingual priest, in a sort-of question-and-answer manner gives these explanations, in a very informal and friendly way.

"The night that I was there, a pilgrim asked about the miracle of the hanged innocent young man that didn't die. I was particularly curious because, frankly, it does take a huge suspension of reason to take the happening anywhere near seriously.

"He [the priest] explained the miracle as a 'modern times' parable, carrying the message that human justice can be, and often is, unjust and wrong, and that human means to dispense it are delicate and could be perilous, and our need to be very careful about it. As a lawyer who occasionally serves as a judge, that explanation has meant very much to me and I share it with my colleagues often.

"The chapel or crypt beneath Santo Domingo's tomb has been renovated and offers a quiet repose in which to rest and meditate, albeit, often, very often, interrupted by the carryings-on of the rooster and his companion just about."

Next to the cathedral is a parador, which has its roots in the humble hospice begun by Santo Domingo. Domingo's hospice was expanded and served as a pilgrim shelter for several hundred years. It was finally abandoned in the 1700s, replaced by the hospital *Convento de San Francisco*. Luckily, the old building was restored in the 1960s and became one of the national paradors.

Church in Santo Domingo de la Calzada.

6 • 9/11 in Santo Domingo de la Calzada

Stunning News from Home

Who knows but the world may end to-night?
—Robert Browning

JOURNAL, DAY 11 (Tuesday, September 11, 2001): **9/11 in Santo Domingo de la Calzada.**

WE WERE AT lunch today when shocking news came on TV; CNN was broadcasting explosions of the Pentagon in Washington, D.C., and at New York City's World Trade Center. Because we didn't understand what was being said, and there were no captions, we initially thought they were airing news of late summer forest fires in the state of Washington. But as we watched the second tower of the World Trade Center explode, and replay after replay of all the events, it became clearer what had occurred. We didn't know who had flown the planes into the buildings.

We were at lunch in a crowded restaurant where most of the people were part of a large, noisy group celebrating a birthday. As the broadcast continued, there were several minutes of quiet as the news was absorbed. But gradually, the celebrants started talking and laughing again. I watched them, wondering how they felt about the turn of events, and whether they supported whoever had done the bombing. But by the end of our meal, which I finished while watching the TV broadcast with tears in my eyes and a lump in my throat, a fellow pilgrim had come over to us to express his sorrow.

WHEN WE WERE told at the refugio that pilgrims could use the Internet service free at Santo Domingo's library, I asked, "Will we need our credentials?"

"No," laughed the host. "They'll recognize you by your sandals." Every night everyone changes from their boots into some other pair of shoes, typically sandals, and we are indeed quite noticeable as we limp and hobble around town.

We found the local library and were promptly given the use of a computer. We logged on the Internet and were able to read a few headlines. It was there that we read that it had been an American Airlines jet flying to Los Angeles that had been hijacked and flown through the World Trade Center towers. It was incredible. We sat there in disbelief.

We learned that all airports had been closed. Though it is more than four weeks until we are scheduled to fly home, we wondered if our flights would be cancelled.

EARLIER IN THE trip I had sent a few e-mails to friends and family at home and had heard back from several. Now, more than ever, we wanted to know that everyone we knew on the West Coast was okay. I was a nervous wreck while waiting for responses to this e-mail:

E-mail to home:
September 11, 2001
Hello everyone,
It is usually wonderful to get news from home, but hearing today's news about the terrorist attacks was terrible! We thought we had nothing to worry about back home—and now we hear of a disaster that's worse than any dreamed up for a movie.

Until now, our pilgrimage has been quiet enough—
traveling on foot from village to village where, initially,
rural life appears to be carried out much as it would
have been a thousand years ago. But our reverie that
Americans are welcome everywhere has now ended.
And the fact that we instantly hear about current events
thousands of miles away, reminds us that we are *not*
living in medieval times.

Today Ralph and I walked twelve-and-a-half miles;
we're more than a quarter of the way to Santiago. Physically, the trip is getting easier for me. Though Ralph
has had NO problems, I have been part of the group (a
large group!) dealing with such problems as sore feet,
legs, and knees. For me, it's been problems with bunions and blisters. However, my feet seem to be getting
tougher; I've had no new blisters for two whole days.

The countryside has changed from the small farms
we saw initially to larger vineyards. Much of the land is
now being burned or turned under because the growing season has come to a close. What remains in the
fields is very healthy-looking, well-maintained crops
of cabbage, beans, tomatoes, and hops.

On a typical day we go through two or three towns
or cities. The smaller ones have no services, but they always have a water fountain, so getting potable drinking
water is no problem. Most of the refugios don't serve
meals, so we are learning where to get food along the
way. For breakfast, we usually get a croissant, coffee,
and tea at the local "BAR." Likewise, the bar is usually
the place to get lunch, though often we pick up bread,
cheese, and meat for picnic fare.

For dinner we usually have the m*enú del dia,* a
fixed-price meal, which costs about twelve dollars for
the two of us. We are served salad or soup or veggies
and a main dish of chicken, beefsteak, fish, etc. Dessert, bread, and wine are included. So the expenses

are not bad at all.

The people we meet on the road, in the cities, and at the refugios are usually quite helpful and friendly. So far we have encountered few who speak English, so we do our best with our limited Spanish. Unfortunately, we're not able to converse with other hikers much in the evenings. (The locals usually do not speak English, and whether or not those staying in the refugios speak English is just a matter of chance.)

Another problem we've encountered is that there seems to be a glut of people traveling through. The refugios are struggling with the increasing number of travelers looking for lodging. And we are always concerned that we will hike all day and then not have a place to stay at night. This has been more worrisome to us than some, I imagine, as we are not the fastest hikers. But we are learning that the people at the refugio will do everything they can to accommodate the pilgrims, and so far we have always found a place to sleep.

This morning we decided to employ the strategy of the others staying at the refugio and get an early start. When the majority of the overnighters started packing at 6:00 AM, we did the same. When they set out at 7:15, we did likewise. We figured we'd have a better chance of arriving with the rest of the pack and of getting a bed in the next refugio. We also thought we'd be able to take a break in the middle of the day and thereby avoid the afternoon heat.

The flaw in our plan was it's still dark that time of morning (sunrise was at almost 8:00 PM). We couldn't see the trail markers. Normally markers are very easy to find and follow (one wonders whether such a system would stay in place in our country).

The actual path on which we travel is varied. Sometimes we are on a dirt, or gravel, or paved surface. Other times the route takes us along the shoulder of a highway or on a sidewalk. We hate highways, not only because of the traffic, but also because it is much harder on our feet. Luckily, we are much more often on the gentle surfaces than the hard ones.

So, though this is not an easy hike, we are learning to trust that things will work out. I hope this letter reflects the state I am in, that is to say, much more optimistic (about finishing the trip) and... that's about it!

Love to all,
Susan and Ralph

I went back to use the Internet at the first opportunity because I wanted updates on the situation back home and to know how our friends and family were faring. Like everyone back home, we wondered who was responsible for the attacks. Word came that thousands had been trapped and killed. Would there be further attacks? What will be the repercussions?

Tue, 11 Sep 2001
Susan and Ralph!!!
With the terrorist (apparently) attacks, it's been quite a day—all the air traffic in the country halted. Major airports closed and evacuated. We haven't started hearing the really sad stuff yet, about people's family members, and all. It seems like thousands of people were affected.

How did you find out about it? Are you reading the news? What does the international press say about all this?

Well—keep trekking . . .
Love, Lorinda and Bob

Tue, 11 Sep 2001
Dear Susan:
...as you know, the news is terrible here...

Best Wishes, Pat

Tue, 11 Sep 2001
Dear Susan,
 . We, here, in the US have been glued to our TV sets, to-
day, as we struggle to comprehend...
Sue Ann

Tue, 11 Sep 2001
I'm in shock and mourning, the whole country is...
Marcy

Tue, 11 Sep 2001
You are thought about often...The situation is scary.
Love, Jean

Tue, 11 Sep 2001
To: "susan alcorn"
Hi Susan & Ralph,

By now you know the sobering news. I just turned on
my computer for the first time in several days and received all three of your e-mails at once. I'm so thrilled at
how wonderfully your trip is going!! Don't let the world
condition dampen your spirits. In fact, let it heighten
your awareness of how wonderful your trip is.
    We're with you in spirit on the trail (and person-
ally I wish I could be there physically, too!). I'll write
again soon.
Much love,
Melanie Clark & Bob

Instantly, in corner bars and small town restaurants, omnipresent TVs blared the news and replayed New York City's
Twin Towers collapsing time and again. Cyber cafes abound,
so even though international phone lines were jammed,

newspapers were scarce (and in Spanish), and planes were brought to the ground, the Internet was a means of quick connection to friends and family at home.

It was difficult being in a foreign country, unable to speak the language beyond the simple phrases to order a meal or ask directions, when our own country was under attack. We wondered what we should do next. Should we sit by the TV awaiting further developments (as many at home did, as it turned out), or should we continue on our journey as planned?

Though I had thought initially that our journey to explore old and new Spain via its historic pilgrimage trail would have many personal physical challenges and spiritual rewards, such as being in nature provides, I didn't expect any incidents of the world-shaking variety. History, however, shows that my expectations of a peaceful stroll uninterrupted by political strife, natural calamities, or criminal activity was myopic. Though 9/11 was unexpected, large-scale disasters and personal incidents affecting pilgrims are not without precedent on the Camino.

HOW COULD IT not be? This is a route that has been traveled for well over a thousand years. It's been undertaken by millions: from the countless, unrecorded pilgrims to such historic characters as Charlemagne, St. Francis of Assisi, Dante, Chaucer, and King Fernando and Queen Isabel (aka Isabella). Its historic importance was recognized officially when it was awarded UNESCO World Heritage site status in 1993. Though, in general, travelers of the Camino de Santiago have completed their pilgrimage without serious mishap, who knows how many have fallen victim to everything from petty pickpockets, disease or illness, warring parties, or murderous highwaymen.

...RALPH AND I continue on.

In the church at Santo Domingo de la Calzada.

7 • Santo Domingo de la Calzada to San Juan de Ortega

Ninety-Nine Bottles of Beer on the Wall

I feel for the common chord again… The C Major of this life.
—Robert Browning

JOURNAL, DAY 12 (*Wednesday, September 12*): **Santo Domingo de la Calzada to Belorado (14 miles/22.5 km).**

WE ALL SLEPT well last night. I didn't hear anyone stirring until seven-twenty. We weren't out the door until after eight, when, theoretically, you are kicked out. We consumed bananas and juice as we walked along. When we reached the next village, we rang the bell of the *panaderia* and went into the bakery's kitchen where we bought two warm *pan chocolate*. Then we went next door to the bar. It was closed, but as we stood there, a middle-aged woman came hurriedly down the street to open up and let us have tea, coffee, and croissants. I certainly wouldn't be able to consume all these delicious pastries if I wasn't getting all this exercise.

We passed through two or three other villages, soaked our feet by a fountain in the middle of one town square, poked our head in a church, and had lunch on steps by a garage.

Because of our late start, we also had more sun with temperatures in the 70s and 80s. Our hike was mostly on a wide, white, sandy-gritty trail just off the highway, with not much of interest. One notable exception was seeing storks' nests; they're oftentimes in the towers of churches. The nests are enormous.

Pilgrims who travel the Camino in the spring or summer are rewarded by seeing the birds themselves. The storks return to their previously-constructed nests in mid-March, lay their eggs, which hatch four weeks later, feed their fledglings for another month, and leave in August for over-wintering in Africa.

We could see the Belorado long before we reached it, which only added to our sense that we'd never get there. When we had just one final kilometer to trudge into town, we began singing *Ninety-nine Bottles of Beer on the Wall*. We managed to get all the way down to thirty bottles. Because we were being boisterous, and because we knew that most of the other pilgrims would not know what we were singing, we found it all very amusing. Sometimes keeping ourselves entertained requires quite a reach!

Belorado is a small town of about 2,000 people. Presently it is suffering from the market declines of its many tanneries and leather manufacturers. Still, this is a good town for hikers to get shoe or boot repairs as well as food and drink..

JOURNAL, DAY 12, resumes: Even in towns that are not particularly attractive, there is always something of interest to find. In Belorado, it is the sandy-looking cliffs and rock formations, which are pockmarked with caves that once housed hermits (the caves are now privately owned). Part of the church holdings appear to be built into the rock, but it's off-limits to us.

We figured we had no chance of finding beds here since we had read there were only thirty-two, but somehow, we found bunks. The showers, toilets, and kitchen, however, are down the street. They put us in the overflow building, the *ayaminato* (city hall), and it has neither water nor electricity. I'm not too impressed with Belorado; it's pretty ugly compared to most towns.

Near our accommodations is a dry canal. While I'm writing this, I'm also watching a very determined cat carry her kittens from one place to another. She has picked up one tiny bundle in her mouth, carried it down the street, down the steep cliff to the dry riverbed (about a ten-foot drop) and then attempted to take it up the other side. Initially, the added weight of the kitten was too much and she was unable to make it up the far slope.

She tried again and failed. Finally, after six attempts, she found her footing and successfully made it to the other side of the canal. She has returned for the second kitten.

We've found out more about the attacks on the U.S., although we'd heard rumors that phone calls from here could not go through. We've heard that 20,000 have died.

Some may wonder how Ralph and I are getting along with all this togetherness. He is very accommodating. For one thing, he has been carrying my sleeping bag, all the food and water, our medical supplies and toiletries almost from the beginning. He also has more energy, or less hobbling to do, at the end of the day, so he goes out, as necessary, to get supplies for the next day's breakfast and lunch.

As we walk, he carries the guidebooks so we know what's upcoming and where the facilities are. Because the terrain the last couple of days has been rather featureless and flat, we can look at a book without stumbling. We've been entertaining ourselves by practicing our Spanish from the phrase book and dictionary as we walk. It's surprising, but we rarely talk about home, future plans, etc.

JOURNAL, DAY 12, *resumes:* I've learned still more about the refugios we stay in. Many are staffed by volunteers; many are people who want to pay back for the experience they had when they walked the Camino. Last night's hosts were a couple who met while walking the trail in 1999. She was from England, he from Holland. In March of this year (2001), they trained for a year's tour of duty. They work seven days a week and up to twelve hours a day during the season.

"Everyone who walks the Camino is surprised at how hard it is," she said.

"Yeah, it's not just me, or just us 'older' ones!" I thought.

She continued, "Many backpackers think they'll have it made, but the day after day, week after week is very different. Recently we had a young man stay here who was a former Israeli soldier. He said that as an army trainee, he had trained with a pack weighing over one-hundred pounds, and he couldn't believe what a difficult time he was having traveling the Camino. He asked me, 'Please don't tell my buddies.' "

It's also very stressful dealing with the language, particularly when we are trying to figure out anything to do with food: where, when, and how to get it. Also not knowing what lies ahead, with both the terrain and accommodations, takes its toll.

But many things are going well. One of the greatest pleasures is meeting and talking with others on the trail. Today we met a man who started from home, in Holland, in March. He went through France, then went home in June to avoid both the hotter weather and summer crowds. Now he is continuing to Santiago with his wife. He has now been on the road a total of 109 days. I think our friend Anna is now too far ahead for us to meet up with her again. Still, at the end of each day, we encounter Pamela and others we know by sight.

We're also happy to be back in sync with the *Lonely Planet's* suggested length of hiking days and their recommended places to stay. In addition, my feet are much better; my leg is okay during the day, and icing it at night seems to help.

Today is the first day I've not taken pain pills for breakfast. The twelve miles of today was much easier than the earliest days; the terrain is gentler, but the heat is more intense.

The next village after Belorado is Tosantos. Soon after, the traveler passes *Ermita de Nuestra Senora de La Pena*, a hermitage dating from the 12th century, which is cut into the rock on the north side of the trail.

Another four miles along is Villafranca de Montes de Oca, a small, but busy town because it's a major truck stop off of the major Highway 120. You'll soon be climbing into the *Montes* (Mountains) de Oca generally following a forest-lined path.

Though the elevation difference between Villafranca Montes de Oca and San Juan de Ortega is only a few hundred feet, the cumulative ascent is greater because of the ups and downs. At the start of one of the steep descents is a small monument, *Monumento de los Caidos*, which marks the location where several dozen Spanish Civil War victims were dumped after being assassinated during a 1936 uprising.

These mountains, now tamed, were once among the more dangerous sections of the Camino. Wolves and bandits preyed on pilgrims making their way through the rugged, forested region. A pilgrim of the 17th century, Domenico Laffi, described seeing mushrooms "as big as a large straw hat."

The trail is now well marked, but Gitlitz and Davidson got lost there as recently as 1974. The changing vegetation, which ranges from heather and broom to forest of pine, is welcome, though heavy logging has left acres of ugly stumps and hacked vegetation.

JOURNAL, DAY 13 (Thursday, September 13): **Belorado to San Juan de Ortega (15 miles/24 km).**

TODAY HAD THE potential of being a great day, but it didn't turn out that way. Because we were going up and into a forested area, I thought it would be a pleasant change. We did notice some changes in vegetation: a lot more heather, ferns, as well as trees. However, the flies were terrible.

At first, I tried swatting at them. That didn't do any good; they were too numerous and too determined. Then we stopped and I sprayed my clothes with Deet; that didn't slow them either. And wouldn't you know it, Ralph was totally ignored! They were so bad that I had to put on my mosquito head-net and wear it through one of the prettiest parts of the walk.

It was not a wilderness area. The pines, oaks, and cypress alongside the trail had been planted in block-formation. The lower branches had been removed, perhaps for fuel and for fire suppression. The trail itself, which is also a logging road, was easy on our feet. At first, the trees provided some shade. Then we came to the vast sections that had been clear-cut for about 20 feet back from both sides of the trail.

When I almost stepped on a snake, it was the last straw. I hate snakes. (The only good thing about it was that it wasn't until after the trip that Ralph read that poisonous vipers were common there.) I fell apart: sobbing and yelling about how awful it all was. Then I stomped off and walked on my own for a while. Ralph called this day "a true relationship test."

We're now in San Juan de Ortega. It's a tiny hamlet that belies its historical importance to the Camino. It was named for San Juan de Ortega, who established a hospice there in the early 1100s. He was born Juan Velazquez in Burgos in about 1080. As mentioned earlier, he became a disciple of (Santo) Domingo de la Calzada and helped him build several bridges. After Domingo died, San Juan went to the Holy Land, but he was shipwrecked on the way home. He prayed to be saved, and promised that if he was, he would forever after help pilgrims en route to Santiago.

San Juan then assumed the lifelong project of developing the path between Villafranca to Burgos, which at the time was an inhospitable stretch of more than twenty miles. He added the name "Ortega" (meaning thistle) presumably because of the abundance in the area. San Juan de Ortega was recognized for his good works during his lifetime and received various grants (including taxes from the region) to help with the enormous task he undertook.

San Juan de Ortega now has a permanent population of only eight according to the *Pilgrim Guide,* but two of its buildings are of interest: its huge church and its once-abandoned monastery. The cathedral has two unusual features. On the ceiling just inside the door are fire-breathing dragons painted in vivid colors. And on the back wall is a large collection of tableaux portraying nude women in adoration of a religious icon.

JOURNAL, DAY 13, resumes: The monastery is now in the process of restoration. The wrought-iron gates across the front are quite spectacular. We stayed in a section of the building allocated for pilgrims. The refugio is typical with bunk beds, and I guess we were lucky to get one. We walked from eight-thirty to three-thirty (with several short stops for our argument). The guidebooks said this walk would take six and a half to seven and a half hours, so I'm pleased that we are within their expected time. Later arrivals are on the floor. The bad thing, however, is no water. Early arrivals had a shower; we haven't. We had to wash our clothes outdoors in the central fountain and hang them near the cathedral and have been using the bathroom in the bar next door. Fortunately, the bar has sufficient beer. Unfortunately, after the bar closes, it will be into the shrubbery for a privy. I took advantage of some free time to record some thoughts about what we've noticed:

Daily life for many of the local people seems to include going to the panaderias, which usually open at about eight in the morning. Bars are often open at that hour also; there one can find not only alcohol and soda, but also coffee, pastries, and bocadillos. Since tapas are so trendy back home, I imagined most bars would have them but it appears they're mostly to be found in the more urban areas.

We see few people outdoors during the day in the towns and hamlets. There are a lot of old-and-new combined buildings and I suspect a lot of the old ones are abandoned or used for animals; we have seen them many places, generally on the outskirts of town, used for housing pigs or chickens.

If the town is large enough, there's lots of activity after five or six in the afternoon. From two to five in the afternoon, it's hard to find anything open. That's the time of the siesta, and no one is on the street except in the larger cities such as Madrid and León. The larger cities are also the only place where you can find Internet/Cyber access.

After the siesta, the older men and women are in the bars playing cards. After six, it's amazing how many people come out. It's hard to get dinner before eight-thirty. There's a lot of activity as evening progresses, but we have to be in the refugio by ten.

There's a division between generations in what the women wear. The older women dress very modestly in rather shapeless dresses; the younger women dress much more stylishly. In the major cities, young women also wear slacks; teenagers often have blue jeans. The men usually wear denims when they are working in the field, but in town they are in cotton shirts, slacks, and cardigan sweaters. Because most of our time has been spent in small villages where the style of dress is more conservative, I have regretted that the only skirt I brought to wear is above the knee.

Hike Your Own Hike

Hike your own hike" is a reminder that each person's pilgrimage will be different. Purists demand that every inch of the Camino be traveled on foot, bicycle, or horseback. The pilgrim office requires only that the last one-hundred kilometers (200 for bicyclists) be completed in that manner. Many think that only staying overnight at pilgrim hostels (the *refugios*) is of merit. Others opt for hotel accommodations arranged by tour companies.

It is always wise to embark on a long distance trek without too many preconceived ideas. There's nothing wrong with having aschedule of miles to travel per day and a list of places to stay each night, but it's better to remain flexible. Opportunities arise and mishaps occur. Sometimes carefully-laid plans should be abandoned when a spot demands more time exploring. Friendships are often forged on the trail; be open to hiking with new companions. Then again, blisters upon blisters or rainy day after rainy day may radically change a traveler's timetable and itinerary. Let the days and nights unfold.

On our Camino trip, we did not allow for unplanned days and later regretted that we had rushed through cities and enchanting locales that deserved more time.

Unplanned may not be the way you are used to traveling. But then, though you may be using vacation time to embark on your Camino journey, it will not be a typical vacation. It will be exhilarating, demanding, exciting, tiring, and rewarding— sometimes all in the same day. It's *life*—with its ups and downs physically, mentally, and spiritually. It may be weeks, months, or years before you are able to completely comprehend just what your experience was all about.

In the Meseta

REGION 3
THE MESETA

Santiago

Astorga

FRANCE

Roncesvalles

Leon

Burgos

• Madrid

PORTUGAL

SPAIN

MOROCCO

Region 3 – The Meseta

• San Juan de Ortega to Burgos	17 miles
• Burgos to Santiago	300 miles
• Burgos to San Bol	14 miles
• San Bol to Itero de la Vega	15.5 miles
• Itero de la Vega to Villalcázar de Sirga	16.5 miles
• Villalcázar de Sirga to Calzadilla de la Cueza	14 miles
• Calzadilla de la Cueza to Bercianos de Real Camino	20 miles
• Bercianos de Real Camino to Mansilla de las Mulas	16.5 miles
• Mansilla de las Mulas to León	11.5 miles
• León to Hospital de Orbigo	22 miles
• Hospital de Orbigo to Astorga	10 miles
• Astorga to Santiago	160 miles

Dovecote on the morning skyline.

8 • San Juan de Ortega to Burgos

Luxury in Burgos

I pity the man who can travel from Dan to Beersheba and cry,
'tis all barren.'

—Laurence Sterne (1713–1768)

JOURNAL, DAY 14 (Friday, September 14): **San Juan de Ortega to Burgos (17 miles/27.5 km).**

TODAY WE GOT off to a good start, leaving about seven-fifteen. The water in the refugio was turned back on at nine-thirty last night, but it was too late for showers. Some people were up at five this morning; this would be easier to deal with if I were a morning person. The first part of the hike was pleasant. We passed through a couple of villages. In one we looked for a fountain in which to soak our feet. There were none, but a woman let Ralph fill our collapsible plastic bucket from her yard and insisted he add two handfuls of salt to it for my poor feet. It did feel good.

We came upon a flock of sheep; they filled the road. We just stood still while they walked past us on all sides. Later, we were passed by a herd of cows. It's much more pleasant to see cows wandering down the lane, or grazing in the field with their bells tinkling, than it is to view them confined by the thousands on bare earth on the large dairy farms and the corporation-owned feedlots back home.

We also went through a bit of forest, happily, no flies! We reached a paved road and followed it to Burgos. When we reached the outskirts of the city, we had to start walking on the concrete sidewalks and follow them to the center of town. After four miles of that, my feet were killing me. But, our trail total for today was seventeen miles, the longest distance so far, so I was proud of that..

Burgos has a population of 170,000; it's been an important city since its founding in 884. It was the capital city of the kingdoms of Castile and León from the 11th to the 15th century and served as the headquarters for Franco's regime from 1936 to 1939.

The legendary El Cid was born near Burgos in 1043, and is clearly still revered there. As you enter the old town section of Burgos on the *Puente* (Bridge) *de San Pablo,* you immediately encounter the larger-than-life statue of El Cid and his horse Babieca, completed by sculptor Juan Cristobal in 1950. The bridge crosses the Rio Arlanzon, the river that El Cid and his men crossed when Alfonso VI exiled him. It's where they set up their tents on the gravel bank.

The Puente de San Pablo has several statues (added in 1955) relating to the history of the Cid. Four are of his fellow warriors of *Poema* fame, four are of his companions, and one is of Dona Jimena.

El Cid

Cid, El Cid, or Cid Campeador, is inextricably tied with Burgos. He is renowned as a Spanish soldier and national hero. He was born Rodrigo Diaz de Vivar in the 1000s and was raised in the court of the Christian ruler Ferdinand I (Fernando). Rodrigo fought under the command of King Ferdinand I when he was trying to establish a unified county, Castilla, as separate from León.

But when Ferdinand died, his will dictated that his vast kingdom be divided among his three sons: Sancho (given Castilla), Alfonso (given León), and Garcia (given Galicia). One daughter, Urraca, was given the city of Zamora; the remaining daughter, Elvira, received Toro.

When Prince Sancho became King Sancho II in 1065, he bestowed the title of "Head of Royal Armies" upon his friend since childhood, Rodrigo. But sibling warfare soon began. King Sancho wanted the kingdom to remain unified; his brothers and sisters resisted. Sancho was assassinated. Alfonso was now King of both Castilla and León. Rodrigo believed (and most sources today agree) that Alfonso had murdered Sancho. He accused Alfonso of the act. When Alfonso declared his innocence, Rodrigo demanded that Alfonso take an oath in the Burgos church of Santa Gadeo saying that he did not slay his brother.

King Alfonso VI took the oath, but declared Rodrigo his bitter enemy and eventually banished him from the county—but not before Rodrigo had married Alfonso's niece, Jimena. Rodrigo then went to serve Zaragoza, a Moorish ruler. (It was not an uncommon occurrence during feudal times for a free lord to thus change his alliance.). In the decade following his banishment from Spain, Rodrigo served for various Christian and Moslem rulers.

The bonds between El Cid and Alfonso were never entirely broken, however. In the 1090s, Rodrigo's troops joined to resist invaders (Berbers) from the east. In 1094, he conquered the region of Valencia and offered it to King Alfonso. Alfonso forgave him for his earlier actions and proclaimed Rodrigo, now El Cid, "Lord of Valencia." Cid ruled Valencia, maintaining a Christian presence, until his death in 1099.

It is said that El Cid never lost a battle. His adventures became much romanticized and the *Poema de mio Cid* (the Song of the Cid) was written during his lifetime. After his death, he was buried in the cathedral at Burgos. Since that time, various plays and ballads have arisen.

JOURNAL, DAY 14, resumes: We are splurging. The *Mesón El Cid* is the finest hotel in the center of town. Our suite has two rooms: a sitting room with sofa and hide-a-bed, table and chairs; and a bedroom with queen bed. Both rooms have a TV with remote. The walls are painted plaster; windows and doors are carved wood. One of the exterior walls opens to an enclosed wooden balcony similar to those we've seen in New Orleans and in Lima, Peru.

Another set of windows opens out towards the courtyard of, and face the main entrance of, the beautiful Burgos Cathedral. The cathedral, which was begun in 1221, dominates the city. It's considered one of the finest examples of Gothic architecture in Europe. Most of the churches and cathedrals that we have seen along the Camino are comparatively dark and massive. The cathedral of Burgos is made of limestone, and its unique filigree spires reach into the sky. The spires are spectacular.

JOURNAL RESUMES: WHEN we first got here, every part of my body—hip joints, legs, and feet—was a mess. Nerves shot and running haywire. After a nap, we both felt better...a *lot* better. I'm sure our staying at this hotel is mostly for me. Ralph could probably put up with the refugio every night of the trip (well, almost, as no one seems to be having sex there. How could you?). I don't miss sleeping in their bunk beds (too hot), especially the top ones, or the cold bathrooms with slippery floors.

We had a good dinner at one of the many nearby cafes. We sampled one of the regional foods, the Burgos Sausage. It's similar to *boudin,* the dark meat sausage with rice in it that we enjoy in Louisiana. I also had filet of beef; I'd rate it two stars, only okay. The flan was good.

Then we walked, in sandals, to the Cyber Café to get more recent news of the attacks on the U.S., the more-recent events, and to read and answer e-mails. I try not to think about the attacks too much because it only makes me feel frustrated and helpless. The news is always in Spanish, so I can't figure out the details. The good news is that it appears that the West Coast has been spared any direct attacks.

Wed, 12 Sept 2001
Hi, Susan & Ralph!
  As you can imagine, everyone here is reeling from the staggering events of yesterday. I wonder how people there are handling it. You are in such a position to hear an international take on it.
  My greatest concern is that we NOT declare war on anybody. There's already heated debate on the radio talk shows (e.g. Michael Krasny this morning) about retaliation against anyone and everyone vs. bringing the specific perpetrators to trial and letting it end there. If we do the former, don't we become what we hate?

Lots of love, Melanie

Wed, 12 Sep 2001
Subject: Re: Sarah and your trip
Dear Susan and Ralph
  Well, Mike and I have no way to leave for Russia—our flight was supposed to be tomorrow on Swiss Air. We were supposed to be back on the 25th with Baby Sarah. Keep us in your prayers; we'll need them!

Karen

Fri, 14 Sep 2001
Dear Susan,
  ...Today we had a National day of prayer and remembrance. There was a lovely service televised from the National Cathedral In Wash. DC. There is a movement for Americans to go out in front of their houses tonight, at 7 p.m., and light a candle of remembrance for the

lives lost, and all affected by Tuesday's tragedy.

Many people are displaying the flag on their homes and autos. It is a very emotional time, but the lovely thing is, we all "feel" more connected.

Sue Ann

Fri, 14 Sep 2001
Hi there,

Hope all is well with you and you're enjoying your trip, even amongst all the recent disasters. I have to honestly say that this is the first time in my life I've ever wanted to own an American flag. By the way, there are none to be found anywhere.

Well, I end this note with love and hopes that your trip isn't tainted in any way and you're enjoying yourselves. See you soon.

Love, Lynn

Fri, 14 Sep 2001
Hi there, Susan and Ralph!

We're thoroughly enjoying your trip from afar! Thanks for including us on your mail list. It's been pretty grim here, as you know. Some of us are trying to show our patriotism in little ways: wearing the red, white and blue, attaching an American flag somewhere, burning a candle in the window, etc. Stories here and there about victims, attempts at rescuing, etc.

I fear what will happen next.... The realization that we really are so vulnerable has hit us. I have such mixed emotions right now... I hope my two boys will live to ripe old ages, and yet I know they are training to serve and protect our country. And for that I am also proud that they have such pride in the U.S.

Anyway, keep trekking! It's nice to hear about your

adventures and refreshing to hear about a topic other than the current one here at home.

May God bless you both....
Sandy

WHEN I READ the e-mails, I felt torn. In some respects I wish I was home with my friends and family, sharing their experiences. Even though most of it is frightening, we could comfort one another. On the other hand, I like the feeling of safety provided by being in (mostly) rural Spain.

And, like most Americans, I enjoy having the freedom to travel where and when I want. Since part of terrorist strategy appears to be to try to instill fear and to disrupt our way of life, I'm happy we're able to go ahead with our original plans. I had been feeling very homesick and worried, so it was good to get word from friends, especially reassurance that they were well, and to receive encouragement to continue our hike.

Still, hiking the trail is almost a surreal experience. When we walk, I often think about the millions who have traveled it and wonder about the number of births, deaths, wars, plagues, marriages, and so forth that have occurred during its 1000-year history.

E-mail to home:
Fri, 14 Sep 2001 13:39:52 -0700 (PDT)
Hello everyone, thank you for update on the attacks on U.S., not pleasant to hear, but it's better than knowing some of what is going on, but not the whole story. The news here is in Spanish and the discussions are too complicated for us to understand with our limited vocabulary.

We've heard from several people whose plans or whose relative's plans were affected by the closure of U.S. airports. Our niece Karen and her husband Mike have had their departure to Russia to pick up the baby they are adopting delayed. It's such a blow, for sure.

We are now in Burgos, which is a major city, and we are splurging on a suite in the finest hotel in town, that is (in my mind) to make up for many days of refugio life: sharing bathrooms and sleeping rooms with 30 or more people—many of whom snore and make bodily noises.

Today was very hard; we went seventeen miles. The weather was cool, which is a plus, but when we reached the outskirts of Burgos, we had to walk on sidewalks for a long way to reach the center of town.

I don't know if I have said, but the people we see mostly are Dutch, French, Spanish, or German; several are from South America. We've met no one from U.S. so far. We take about the same time as many others to cover a certain distance, so we meet up with many of the same people for several days in a row.

We are discussing busing across the meseta, which is about 80 miles of grueling, arid land. We shall see. It would take six or seven days to walk it, a couple of hours if we take a bus.

We have now finished approximately 162 miles (270 kilometers). I appreciate your letters because it is never a walk in the park; it's really tough for me. Ralph, on the other hand, is doing great (and carrying my sleeping bag and all the other heavy things I can palm off on him). He's champing at the bit; he wants me to end this, so I will.

I cry only every third day now. After talking to others, I find my feelings are typical.

Love, Susan

Burgos is a university town and the bars, cafes, and streets are often crowded until two in the morning. What a contrast to the quiet hamlets where everyone shuts off the lights at nine and you feel guilty if you read in bed.

I feel like a little girl from the country coming to the big city and seeing the dazzling lights for the first time. It's so exciting to see stores and shops with clothing and shoes and jewelry for sale after being in the rural areas for the last several days.

We will stay an extra day here and then decide whether to walk, or bus, to León. When we arrived here I was exhausted, but now that I've showered, washed my clothes and eaten, I feel ready to walk again. It's very confusing.

JOURNAL, DAY 15 (Saturday, September 15): **Second day in Burgos.**

WE SLEPT IN, then had wonderful pastries, freshly-squeezed orange juice, and our tea and coffee. We toured the Burgos Cathedral though the main sanctuary was closed due to renovations. The incredible carvings, paintings, and especially, marble sculptures certainly demonstrate the dedication and religious nature of the people. The trims and columns of the cathedral all have unique carving.

ANOTHER HIGHLIGHT TODAY was watching several wedding parties that followed weddings in both the cathedral directly across the plaza from us and the church on the left side of the plaza. The gowns were all quite beautiful, and most of the guests were richly attired: lots of gorgeous silks and satins, the grooms in cutaway jackets or well-tailored suits. The affairs were decidedly more formal that we generally see back home these days, and it was wonderful to see.

I enjoyed seeing confetti and rice being thrown, even though I know it's not considered environmentally correct. Hours after the weddings, the talking, greetings, and hugs continued. Then we watched the various wedding parties move to the fountain on the plaza or to a grassy area by the park to continue with photos.

RALPH ACCOMPANIED ME without complaint when I decided I wanted to send and check my e-mail messages again.

> E-mail home
> Sat, 15 Sep 2001
> Hello everyone,
> Today was a much-needed respite for me, and Ralph didn't mind a rest either. Burgos was a wonderful, pleasant surprise to me. The city is very cosmopolitan, with fine shops with tremendous selections. We visited the Burgos Cathedral and couldn't help but admire the incredible artwork and craftsmanship. It continues to amaze that even the most remote village (as well as this major city) has an immense cathedral demonstrating enormous dedication and effort towards celebrating or worshiping the divine.
> Because our hotel overlooks both the cathedral and a church on the central plaza, we were able to watch several wedding parties today. The brides were beautifully dressed, with long trains and elaborate veils. The guests rose to the occasion and were wearing very elegant clothes—much dressier than we Americans typically are today.
> Since we are wandering the city with our boots and hiking clothes, we will not be invited to receptions. However, I think the Spanish are much more accepting than we are in many ways. For example, whereas here we might look askance at someone very sweaty, with a backpack, coming into our finer hotels, they are very hospitable.
> I loved being able to get up when I wanted today, having full-size towels (yes, Jean, I am still carrying only the smallest containers of lotions, toothpaste, etc. and my "towel" is about twelve inches square all in order to save weight), and having a bar of soap instead of a scrap. I've missed the everyday pleasures of soaking

in a clean bathtub, reading in bed, and sleeping in the nude. And not only do we get to choose our own bedtime, I don't have to listen to anyone snoring, except Ralph occasionally, and I can push him over!

We will set off tomorrow for a long (maybe six to seven days) section of the walk during which we will probably not have opportunity to write again. The next major stop is León.

Love to all, Susan and Ralph

Sat, 15 Sep 2001
Dear Susan,

I've watched TV and listened to National Public Radio (NPR) a lot. So many stories. This tragedy keeps unfolding. So much to absorb. Nearly 5000 people missing from the twin towers of New York—about 200 from the Pentagon. So much debris everywhere, not to mention the soot and smoke that continues to rise from the N.Y. site. The collapse of the towers created a racing explosion of debris and soot that engulfed people as they raced from the scene. Americans bought out flags from stores so that no supplies remained.

There has been a tremendous outpouring of compassion from all over the nation plus services telecast from many foreign countries. I've heard our national anthem sung by many nations. The workers continue at a frantic pace trying to remove rubble hoping beyond hope that some people might still be alive. They work beyond exhaustion refusing to leave the scene. People who are missing loved ones carry and post the pictures of them everywhere. And they tour every one of the many hospitals in N.Y. hoping to find a loved one.

Susan, it has been so horrendous. The rescue workers and firemen continue to be the heroes but everyone has been pitching in. Bush has declared war on the terrorists and is soliciting help from many nations.

Love, Donna

15 Sep 2001
Susan and Ralph,
We wish you were back here with us! As you can imagine, we are all very shaken by the events on Tuesday; the numbness is wearing off and a myriad of other feelings are creeping in. I've noticed that the traffic is much less aggressive than usual—people are raw, tender. No one is unaffected. We want to gather around us the people we care about.

If you were here, we could get together and have beer, or custard pie, or something else we like, and share one another's company...but since we can't, then keep having fun (if you call that fun, Susan, crying every third day)!

Love,
Lorinda and Bob

Burgos has long been important as a pilgrimage city; in the 1500s, it had 32 pilgrims' hospitals—more than any other town on the Camino. Today there is a large refugio (capacity about 100) on the outskirts of town as well as a wide range of other accommodations.

JOURNAL, DAY 15, resumes: We walked about a mile through the city streets to reach the local refugio on the outskirts of town. We wanted to get our certificates stamped and to see if we could find anyone there whom we knew. The refugio is composed of several new wooden barracks. They're very clean, but crammed with bunk beds. I'm really glad we had our day's respite at the hotel.

SPAIN IN GENERAL comes to life at night in the large towns and cities; Burgos is no exception. It has finally cooled off, siesta is over, and it's time to shop and see friends. We enjoyed the throngs of people, and a good meal. After a bowl of soup and a serving of trout, I was too full to have dessert. I solved that problem, though: I brought a delectable cream puff filled with whipped cream back to our room. The food here is so good you wish you could figure out a way to hold more.

Approaching Castrojeríz.

9 • Burgos to Mansilla de las Mulas

Nueve meses de invierno
y tres de infierno.

—Miguel de Cervantes (Don Quixote)

From Burgos to Astorga the traveler is on the *meseta*—a region often described as "nine months of winter and three of hell (*nueve meses de invierno y tres de infierno*)." This elevated plateau, ranging from 1300 feet (400m) to 3300 feet (1000m) in the heart of Spain, covers forty-percent of the country. The eastern boundary of the meseta is the *Sistema Iberico*, which you climb before entering Burgos. To the south the meseta extends beyond Madrid to the *Sierra Moreno* and almost to Andalucia. The northern edge is bounded by the *Cordillera de Cantábrica*, and northwestern is formed by the *Montes de Leon*, over whose peaks and passes the pilgrims climb to reach Galicia.

WEATHER IN THIS inland region can be unbearably hot or freezing cold. During the summer there is little shade in this hot, dry land; during the winter there is little to shelter you from the frigid winds that sweep across the (largely) treeless plain.

JOURNAL, DAY 16 (Sunday, September 16): **Burgos to Arroyo de San Bol (14 miles/23 km).**

THE HOTEL NEGLECTED, or misunderstood, our request for a wake-up call, but we still got underway from Burgos at seven-thirty. We were lucky; most of the morning was cool and breezy. I had to keep my fleece cap on, but just a long-sleeved shirt over my tee-shirt was enough.

Just on the outskirts of Burgos, we heard shotgun shots, and saw a Roe doe and fawn running across the fields. They're small, white-tailed, and reddish: the kind of deer you'd expect to see in English paintings with such titles as "The Hunt," or "The Stag."

We made fairly good time today, largely because walking on the more level terrain is not very strenuous. We're seemingly out in the middle of nowhere; the nearest municipality, the village of Iglesias, is three miles away. However, the fact that there is a river nearby apparently made it a good site for the former monastery, San Baudillo, which was founded here in the mid-1000s.

The present-day refugio at Arroyo de San Bol is modern and unique. As we approached the building we saw that one end of the building was rather ordinary looking with straight exterior walls and sloping roof, but the other end had a dome-shaped ceiling. A red cross had been painted on the white-washed wall under the dome. We rounded the building to the entrance and were intrigued to find that the walls were covered with murals. The murals portrayed nude people in a variety of poses; I'm not sure early pilgrims would have approved of them.

We were warmly welcomed and led through the kitchen/dining area to the sleeping room. After we claimed our beds, we went back through the main room and peeked into the dome at the far end. John Brierley, in A *Pilgrim's Guide to the Camino de Santiago,* states that a small group of people attracted to the ideals of the Knights Templar renovated this site. The inside of the dome has been painted with a dark-blue background and with stars on top. Several incense burners had been set on a narrow ledge that runs around the circumference of the chapel. I was grateful they were not lit because the smell would have given me an instant headache.

There is a big concrete trough behind the refugio, fed by a natural spring. It essentially has become a pool. The water is said to heal your feet for the rest of your journey to Santiago. We gave it a try. The water was so cold that my feet quickly changed from feeling like blocks of wood to feeling like blocks of ice. But other than the pool, there is no water—nor is there plumbing or electricity. To go to the bathroom, we have to go out beyond the trees into a large field. I made a visit into the field; toilet paper was strewn everywhere. I hope I don't have to come out here after dark.

A German couple, with whom we talked at lunch, have arrived. Both were very excited to see the pool. They soon stripped and jumped in. She shrieked when she hit the water; it is so cold I think I would have had a heart attack if I'd tried it. He didn't yell. but he also didn't spend a long time in the water.

Malu, our friend from Brazil, arrived soon after the couple. After she found a bed, and I washed and hung out my laundry, we all found a place to sit on the outdoor benches. I leaned against the refugio's sun-baked walls and surveyed the nearby golden fields, poplars, and gentle rolling hills. As the sun's descent began to turn my surroundings dark amber, I headed for the nearby woods and practiced some Chi Gong and yoga stretches and poses.

Our host prepared dinner with ingredients brought out by local people earlier in the day. It cost an extra three dollars each (on top of the accommodations) to have dinner here, but if we hadn't purchased it, we'd have had to do without since there is nothing else here. We had ample to eat. We were served lentil soup and spaghetti with seconds on both. The wine was a different matter. Our host brought out a bottle of red, but instead of pouring it directly into our glasses, he carefully measured some into a cup, then poured our allotment into our glasses.

In spite of his penny-pitching manner of pouring libations, I liked our host. We were intrigued by the fact that he has been here every summer for five years, two of them alone. I had to admire his competence; it can't be convenient for him to operate with no running water. He's lucky to have the spring nearby.

Our host and all the other guests, except Malu and us, were German. We would have heard only their native language all night, if it were not for the fact that a couple (whom Ralph had helped earlier by supplying bandages for their blisters), and the host, sat down with us for dinner.

Our table companions expressed their opinions about the terrorist attacks on the United States. This was the first opportunity we've had to hear anyone say anything.

"We are brothers; we are part of the Western world," our host announced emphatically. "My country's as vulnerable to attack as yours was," he said.

"I have great respect for the Americans," he continued. "My father was seventeen when he joined the military during WWII. In 1945, as the war was winding down, he was captured by the U.S. forces and became a POW; he was only nineteen. When the Americans ran out of food for the prisoners, they released him." Our host's underlying conviction was strong; his father would not have fared as well if any other army had captured him.

I am looking forward to a relaxing overnight stay here. Since there are only a dozen people here, it seems much more intimate. And because our dinner conversation was congenial rather than hostile, I feel more comfortable being surrounded by strangers.

I MADE A couple of observations today unrelated to the passing scenery. I realized that loosening my shoestrings has given my swollen feet more room to expand. It remains to be seen, but at the moment it appears that I have been lacing my shoes too tightly all along, and it has caused me much grief. Secondly, I don't think I have lost an ounce of weight. How depressing!

JOURNAL, DAY 17 (Monday, September 17): **Arroyo de San Bol to Itero de la Vega (15.5 miles/25 km).**

EVERYONE SLEPT IN, comparatively speaking, at San Bol this morning. It was still dark when Ralph and I got up. We were only the third and fourth people to depart. The wind was howling.

Today was long. We are well into the meseta now, but it's not so bad. It's nothing like I had feared for months before the trip. And, it's not totally flat. There are rolling hills nearby; in fact, we had to go up one steep grade today. There is little that's green; the landscape is golds and tans.

But, there is always something of interest. Today it was a vast field of sunflowers, their enormous golden heads all pointed towards the sun, creating the sort of scene that inspired Van Gogh. Other times it's the wild grasses blowing in the wind, or the bleached stubble of harvested crops, or the contrasting swathes of dark, disked soil. Even out here, we still occasionally encounter large flocks of sheep.

In a way, I think with the less colorful and varied surroundings I notice and appreciate the subtle differences even more. This is definitely "living in the moment." We're finding that our minds are pretty free of anything but walking, food, and shelter.

On our route between San Bol and San Antón, we passed through the town of Hontanas, which Domenico Laffi, during his pilgrimage in the 1670s, described as "small, wretched, and poor." In those days Hontanas was nothing more than a dozen or so huts occupied by shepherds. Laffi warned that the only safe time to pass through the region was when the shepherds' huge dogs were out affording some protection. Otherwise travelers were at the mercy of wolves that dotted the landscape like "flocks of sheep" day and night.

THE RUINS OF a monastery at San Antón date from the 1300s. If the arch (under which the highway nowadays passes) is any indication, the former buildings were quite beautiful. The abandoned Convent of San Antón cared for pilgrims with San Anthony's Fire: a disease with symptoms similar to leprosy. The convent provided exercise, red wine, and spiritual comfort. Wayfarers arriving late in the day would find food left by the monks in niches in the convent's outer walls; modern pilgrims still leave notes offering prayers, or comfort, under stones.

THE *PILGRIM GUIDE* suggests Julius Caesar may have founded Castrojeríz. As we passed through the small village, we noticed a crypt marker with two skulls and crossed bones on one of the outer walls of the Iglesia de Santo Domingo; the Latin inscription translates to *death* (over one skull) and *eternity* (over the other).

Gitlitz and Davidson inform us that the neighboring mesa was fortified at least from the Celtiberian times and that (perhaps two centuries later) the Romans used this vantage point to protect the road to the Galician gold mines.

The castle atop the hill was built in the Middle Ages, replacing an earlier one from pre-Roman times. More recently a private family owned it. Hikers who enjoy a steep climb can visit the castle's ruins; from the hilltop they will have a clear view, both literally and figuratively, of *why* this location was such a strategic one.

Cut into the hillside are many underground cellars, *bodegas,* which are manmade and currently in use. Although some have chimneys, they are not for habitation, but for cold storage of produce and wine. Most are single-room caves, but some have been constructed with many interconnected underground rooms.

AN EASIER TOUR may be had of the *Ex-colegiata de Santa María del Manzano.* This church is believed to be the site of several miracles. In their *Pilgrimage Road to Santiago,* Gitlitz and Davidson relate that "Several of the miracles described in the

Cantigas [religious songs written by Alfonzo X] have to do with this church's construction."

The Miracles at Santa María del Manzano

As Santiago was traveling through, he thought he saw an image of the Virgin in a *manzano* (apple) tree. He leaped onto his horse and in so doing, his horse's hoofprint was left in a rock. Contemporary visitors may be interested in viewing the print, which is near the church's entrance.

"*Cantiga* 242 tells how a man slipped while working on one of the vaults, and how the Virgin gave him strength to hold on by his fingertips. *Cantiga* 249 tells how another mason, who worked not for salary but for love of the Virgin, was saved from a fall. *Cantiga* 252 tells of workmen "digging the foundation to the 'church called Almazon, at the edge of the town,' the sand caved in, killing many of them, but that when the survivors prayed to the Virgin their colleagues were resuscitated. Finally, *Cantiga* 266 recounts how when workmen were putting up scaffolding to build the tower and main portal a large falling beam would have crushed them if the Virgin had not held it up." (Gitlitz and Davidson, pg. 202)

JOURNAL, DAY 18 (Tuesday, September 18): **Itero de la Vega to Villalcázar de Sirga (16.5 miles/27 km).**

THIS MORNING AS we started out of town, we saw our first *palomares* (dovecotes). These adobe structures, set in the middle of the fields, are for doves. They're either rectangular or round and are usually soundly constructed because of their importance. Doves sit inside the buildings on rows of roosts. Their droppings supply fertilizer and the birds themselves provide bug control and, ultimately, Sunday night's dinner.

In Boadilla del Camino's town center, we saw the *Rollo* (gibbet) *de Boadilla*. The *gibbet* is a judicial post dating from the 16th century. It was bad news for criminals of the time; they hung there until animals disposed of them.

I'VE BEEN MENTALLY rehearsing what I'd like to tell friends at home about what I'm learning about stress and worry. "Hi, everyone. This experience has given me ample opportunity to observe that my bad habit of worrying is usually counter-productive. When we were planning and getting ready for the trip, I found countless things to be concerned about. The meseta had been described as unrelentingly flat and featureless. But, in reality, it has been interesting in its own way. I'm finding that adopting a 'We'll just deal with it' (whatever comes up) attitude is much more helpful. Stressing about things that most likely won't ever happen, or getting upset about things over which I have no control (such as having to wait in line or not finding an empty bed) is a ridiculous waste of energy."

WE HAVE NOW completed three days of the meseta; we have come to enjoy it. The first and second days were somewhat windy, but the breezes were usually welcome because they kept the temperature down. The third day, yesterday, was extremely windy; at times I struggled against the wind, which seemed determined to push me and my pack over sideways. Though I wouldn't want to live with the wind blowing constantly, it isn't so bad for traveling through.

I like the way it provides an opportunity to "go within" and meditate on life. Today, as we were talking about the rarity of seeing wildlife, speculating that the farmers probably shot anything that moved, a heron rose out of the canal alongside us and gracefully flew across the field to a row of trees. Smaller birds, startled, came out of the trees, and started diving at him.

Though the meseta appears flat, watercourses cut through it. In the mid-1700s, several canals were built through the region, providing water for villages and agriculture. Mid-morning we passed through Frómista. Its Romanesque church, *San Martín*, is considered one of the finest in Spain. The church itself is built of cut stone blocks. It has more than 300 carved figures, each one unique, around the edge of the roof. The church was heavily restored in about 1900; many purists decry the changes, but it is still wonderful in its simplicity. The original interior was most likely covered with brilliantly-colored frescos; today the walls are unpainted.

JOURNAL, DAY 18, resumes: Later on we came upon a flock of sheep moving towards us on the road. We stood still as they approached and waited while the group split to walk around us. Neither they, nor their alert sheepdogs, bothered us. At first we were apprehensive upon seeing the dogs; we had read warnings about dangerous ones along the path. But we've not had any problems, nor has anyone else we've talked with. We're applying some common sense: we make sure not to get too close to the sheep, or to get between the dog and the sheep. (We follow similar precautions when we are backpacking in the mountains of California; we avoid bear encounters, particularly situations where we could get between a mother bear and her cubs.)

WE MOVED FAST across the meseta. Nevertheless, the small villages of the meseta are a welcome sight, especially at the end of the day. The small refugio in Villalcázar de Sirga (which will close for the season within the next week) is no exception. There are nine beds and they're not stacked.

As the day wore on, it had become more difficult for me. By the time we arrived here, the plantar fasciitis of my right foot was acting up and my body was hurting all over. I jumped into the shower hoping warm water would relax my aching muscles. I hit the water control faucet and soon found myself chilled from the combination of low-flow water and the cold concrete floor. Once again I swore at my towel. A 12-inch square of fleece-like material, no matter how absorbent, does not cut it. How I miss my fluffy terry bath towels back home! It took over an hour wrapped up in my sleeping bag to end my shivering.

I'm feeling lonely. Obviously many of the other hikers are on a different schedule than we are, and have either stayed further back or ahead of us the last couple of days. We are with a completely new set of people; we've gotten out of sync with familiar faces (such as Malu's). The fact that there's a group of friends traveling together here who are having a party—cooking dinner together, enjoying wine, and laughing—only accentuates that we are outsiders. Earlier today, I figured out *how* (there have been few phones and we don't have calling cards) and *when* (taking into account the time difference) to call Mom. Now I'm too upset to want to talk to anyone.

Anticipating a special dinner helped me make the effort to get out of my sleeping bag. One of our guidebooks described the restaurant *Mesón de Pablo* as excellent. We looked forward to a terrific meal and service. We entered through the front door and then pushed through heavy, drawn drapes that not only cut down on what would otherwise be a drafty room, but also provided a break between modern day outside and pilgrim setting inside. The walls were decorated with pilgrim clothing and accoutrements.

Atmosphere we got, but we were very disappointed with the cool treatment given us by the waiter, and though the food was good, we did not think it exceptional.

JOURNAL, DAY 19 (Wednesday, September 19): **Villalcázar de Sirga to Calzadilla de la Cueza (14 miles/23 km).**

WHEN ALARM CLOCKS started going off at four-thirty this morning, it did not bode well. The host had asked when we wanted breakfast, and we said seven-thirty, but when we went down to have some, she wasn't there. Coffee and tea, along with some leftover cookies, were available in the kitchen. We ate our apples and bananas, then left.

We stopped for coffee, tea, and croissants in Carrión de los Condes, three miles along. It's described as having all facilities, so I was looking forward to using the Internet, and Ralph wanted to get cash at the bank. He found the bank, but we couldn't find a computer. We walked on.

Carrión de los Condes, according to the *Pilgrim Guide*, was once a town of 12,000. It is reputed to be the place where Moorish overlords forced the Christians to surrender 100 virgins each year. When the Christians prayed for an end to this carnage, Santa María released a herd of bulls to drive off the Moors. The scene is depicted on the portal of the *Iglesia de Santa María del Camino*.

Nowadays quiet Carrión de los Condes, with its present day population of 3,000, lies in the midst of a vast agricultural area. It's a good place to pick up food and water for the long dry stretch ahead until Sahagún.

JOURNAL, DAY 19, resumes: Then we had one of our biggest arguments of the trip; I'm still not sure why. I can wonder about that because I was the one who caused the argument, and I set it up purposefully. I had stated last night that I was tired and upset and wanted to walk only to the next town, Carrión, and stay over. I was upset not only because of the long walk, but also because we were among strangers, and there was no privacy when I just wanted to be held and have a good cry. This morning, Ralph asked how I felt, and when I said, "Fine," he thought it meant we would go on as if nothing had happened; I was still expecting to rest.

So when we found ourselves walking through town, and then continuing on the trail, with Ralph never checking about whether I still wanted to stay over or not, I chose to not say a word until we were some distance down the pike. *Then* I let him have it! The ensuing discussion was productive, I think, as he realized his fault in not checking with me, and I definitely knew I was playing the martyr. The question that remains for me is why I didn't just ask for the comfort that I wanted since I know he would have provided it.

It was a long, boring, hot day on a straight track to Calzadilla de la Cueza. The only good thing about the trail was that the surface was of crushed gravel, which makes for more comfortable walking.

MY SPIRITS IMPROVED dramatically when we reached the *Hostal Camino Real* and we were cordially welcomed. Then the owner carried my bag up the two flights of stairs. He refused to take our ID, let us register, or pay any money until we were comfortably settled. He made it clear he welcomed and trusted pilgrims.

"*Mas tarde,*" he waved, "pay later." It's a very clean and comfortable hotel. Although it's unheated like all the rest, it has the best shower yet. We should be celebrating because according to the guidebook, *we are more than halfway* to Santiago.

JOURNAL, DAY 20 (Thursday, September 20): **Calzadilla de la Cueza to Bercianos de Real Camino (20 miles/32.5 km)**
We left after breakfast at 8:00. Midday, we stopped in Sahagún and had lunch in a comfortable hotel restaurant. We found a shop for using the Internet. Since I had about 25 messages, it took some time.

The proprietor of the Internet shop didn't say anything for a while, then, in fluent English, told us that they normally closed at two o'clock for the siesta; it was already two-thirty. We promised to be quick, and he graciously said, "No problem." After he locked up, we all started out in the same direction. When we came to the beautiful stone arch that is an entrance to the city, he offered to take a picture of Ralph and me together. We continue to meet kind people.

> E-mail home to Melanie
> Thu 20 Sep 2001
> Dear Melanie,
> Yes, we are walking now, still considering a bus at some point, but shall see. I had totally dreaded the meseta as it is described as nine months of winter, and three of Hell, but I think we sort of slipped in between these two extremes. Some is pretty bleak, but mostly it is like walking across Kansas (not that I've done this, but my impression). It sort of forces you to look for the little differences—a flower, a flock of sheep, pattern in the

fields. We are both feeling better in general, though at the same time sort of fighting colds.

We totally agree with your thoughts on war. We definitely share your concern about how we would define the enemy. And most people we talk to (not an American to be seen yet) agree also. But they do say, "We are your brothers, we support you (the U.S.)."

Love, Susan

Sahagún today belies its importance during the height of Camino pilgrimage. It was then the most important Benedictine monastery in Spain. Nowadays, it's a small, modern town of less than 3,000 people. Much of the original monastery and other churches of the town are now gone or in ruins, but the accommodations for contemporary pilgrims in the *Albergue Municipal* adjacent the *turismo* (tourist office) are said to be excellent. There is also a campground near the Cea River with a swimming pool.

JOURNAL, DAY 20, resumes: We continued on our way, expecting to stay overnight about three miles out of Sahugún in Calzada del Coto. When we reached the small village of Calzada del Coto, we considered how we felt, and since nothing hurt, and we weren't particularly tired, we decided to go on.

Just 300 meters before Calzada del Coto is an important trail junction for pilgrims. There are the two routes: the *Real* (Road) *Camino Francés* for walkers and bicyclists and the *Calzada de los Peregrinos,* which is suitable for hikers only. We took the *Real Camino Francés.* While the alternate trail is a more authentic, mainly the Roman route, it is also rougher. Also, about thirteen and one-half miles (22 km) of that twenty mile (33 km) route has no shade, water, or facilities.

JOURNAL RESUMES: YESTERDAY we puzzled over a section of trail where the trees were planted on the north side of the trail. We can't figure any rationale for planting on that side; the trees are deciduous, so they won't be able to protect hikers during the winter, and the sun is mostly from the south, so the trees won't be able to protect hikers during the summer. Maybe someone made a mistake? Nevertheless, we are enjoying the liquidambers (sweet gum) as they are just now coming into their beautiful fall colors of red and gold. Trees along its southern edge paralleled today's trail. Makes more sense to me because that allows the trees to provide shade to travelers.

WE ARRIVED IN Bercianos de Real Camino at four-thirty. We appear to be the only guests here at the *Hostal-Restaurante Rivero*. Great for us, bad for them. The rooms are very clean and comfortable.

After we were settled in our room, we went for a walk to check out the local refugio. The *Pilgrim Guide* said, "Avoid, unless stuck—no beds, no running water." While it's true there are no beds, there are both thick sleeping mats and running water. There were no more than a half-dozen people staying over. No matter, for about $30, we are enjoying privacy, warm showers, large towels, and a shared bed.

Though we recognized a few hikers from earlier on the trail and saw several bicyclists as well, we've concluded that the maelstrom of people is now ahead of us. Hooray! (It's also possible that most took the alternate route.) One of the bicyclists staying here is now heading home to Belgium after touring Europe for more than five months.

When it was dinner time, we headed back to the hostel. The manager picked up the phone and called a woman from down the street to come and prepare our meal. We were the only ones dining.

We calculated our mileage for today: more than nineteen miles. We couldn't believe it at first, so we double-checked our figures. We didn't plan to go that far, had not included the mileage of one nine-mile segment. Strangely, we don't feel as tired as we are most days. This isn't unusual for many on the trail, but it sure is for us. I think it's due to our increased strength and stamina, no limping on my part, the good trail and weather.

Most of the day we were on a dirt trail rather than paved surfaces. And whereas yesterday was so hot that we could see heat waves on the land, today was cooler because of an overcast sky. I had been concerned that our lengthy stop in Sahagún would put us behind schedule. As it turned out, the long break was refreshing and now we'll have a shorter hike tomorrow.

Tonight I will check for e-mails from friends. Much of the time while what we are walking on what has been almost a straight track across the meseta, I compose letters to people back home. When I actually get to an Internet café, however, I find that the pictures I want to paint take too long.

Thu, 20 Sep 2001
To: "susan alcorn"
Dear Susan,
  I'm afraid of Bush plunging ahead. I'm in favor of a solution without the declaration of war. Am afraid of innocent people being killed. The "Towers" number of dead is now over 6,000.*
  Glad you're still seeing many sights on your hike. You will have to write a book.
  Blessings,
  Donna

*DONNA'S NOTE THAT 6,000 had died in the Twin Towers is just one example of the difficulty, even in these days of instant electronic communication, of obtaining accurate information during emergency circumstances. As of August 8, 2004, the total number of deaths from the bombings—including those in the World Trade Center, the Pentagon, and the four airliners—was 2,996. Confirmed are 2,948 dead; reported dead 24; missing 24. (www.september11victims.com).

Journal, Day 21 (Friday, September 21): **Bercianos de Real Camino to Mansilla de las Mulas (16.5miles/27 km).**

WELL, IT RAINED for a short time last night so we set out today prepared for more. We lined our backpacks with plastic bags and kept our rain clothes at the ready. Most of the day it looked as if it would rain momentarily, but it didn't start until we were about a mile from our stopping point here in Mansilla. By that time we'd had a hot spell and changed to shorts. Luckily it was a light rain and an umbrella was sufficient. With the high humidity it would have been very uncomfortable with full rain gear.

Today's distance traveled was shorter than yesterday's with somewhat more diversity in terrain. Most of the time we walked on an eight-foot wide track of dirt covered with gravel. We had plowed fields and corn to look at.

Huge picnic tables have been installed alongside the trail as part of a campaign to accommodate 21st century pilgrims wending their way to Santiago. With little else to do while walking, Ralph entertained himself by counting the distance between the similarly-installed concrete benches. Most were 700 to 900 paces apart. I continued to compose letters and questions for friends and family.

Tonight at dinner we met an English couple who translated the news for us. Apparently Bush is saying he wants Bin Laden turned in or he will bomb Afghanistan, Pakistan, and Iraq. Makes no sense to us at all.

Ralph and I both now have colds with sore throats now. He also has a cough, so neither of us slept well last night. Luckily, he feels okay when he is up and about, or so he says. The hostel here in Mansilla de las Mulas is not very fancy but seems clean enough. The bath is down the hall. By staying here, those at the town's refugio are spared a sleepless night from Ralph's coughing.

The two routes that formed back before Calzada del Coto rejoin at Mansilla de las Mulas. This town dates from Roman times and was laid out in typical style with its streets forming a grid with a central plaza that held the church and governmental buildings. During the Middle Ages, additional walls were constructed to further protect the city. Many of those walls remain as well as some of the gates. The name *Mansilla* can be translated from *mano* to hand and *silla* to saddle; the town's coat of arm shows a hand resting on a saddle, but in our Lonely Planet guidebook, *Walking in Spain*, they suggest that it might be derived from *mansionella* because of its origins as a Roman *way-station*. *Mulas* means mules. That dates from earlier times: when mules were raised in the area and sold in the town's marketplace.

Pilgrim Monument.

10 • Mansilla de las Mulas, León, to Astorga

León and the Cathedral with No Walls

A thing of beauty is a joy for ever...

—John Keats

JOURNAL, DAY 22 (Saturday, September 22): **Mansilla de las Mulas to León (11.5 miles/ 18.5 km).**

WE LEFT MANSILLA de las Mulas this morning just after 8:00. It had rained during the night, but luckily the only significant rain of the walk occurred at one of the mid-way points. We ducked into a bar for tea and coffee while waiting for it to let up.

It was amusing to see how different people dealt with the rain. A couple ahead of us had on rain ponchos that not only covered them from head to toe but also covered their backpacks. I, on the other hand, had concluded that it was so warm that a jacket or parka would reduce me to a pool of sweat, and elected to stay with my long-sleeved underwear top, a short sleeve shirt layered over it, shorts, and my umbrella. I was perfectly comfortable, and quite pleased that all I had to do when it stopped raining was put away my umbrella.

León is a gorgeous city. When you look up the avenue *Ancha*, you see what has to be one of the grandest avenues of Europe. Beautiful old shops and stores line the pedestrian walkway lead-

131

ing to the Cathedral (which we plan to visit tomorrow). We are staying at the *Hotel Paris* (yes, another one!), which is near the center of town and the Camino's route.

I'm so happy that I can call Mom tonight from the hotel. The combination of different time zones, non-compatible phone systems, and not having the equivalent of twenty dollars in pesetas has prevented us from calling before. We've also checked on the status of airlines; we've found that flights to the U.S. have resumed, so we think we will be able to get home on schedule.

Last night Ralph sat upright much of the night so he would not cough, but as a result did not sleep very much. It feels very luxurious to be in a hotel, with a bed and bath, and to be able to "fool around."

We went out about six this evening. Things were coming to life; the stores were reopening and will be full of shoppers until ten or later. In the small towns, small groups would be gathering at this time in the bar—men to play cards, women the same (or maybe to crochet while sitting on their doorsteps). Then the groups would disperse as the dinner hour approached. The bar would open a back room, or set some tables at 8:30 or so for customers wanting to order the set menu or ala carte.

Here, we ate at the dining room of our hotel. Though there were other couples, most tables were occupied by groups of four: either men or women. The women were neatly dressed in suits, nylons, and heels. Their animated conversations were interrupted only by their frequent sips of hot coffee and Nescafé. The men were also conservatively dressed: wearing double-breasted, shiny-seated, wide-lapelled suits. I'd love to be able to ask if they typically meet with their friends daily, weekly, or monthly.

WE'RE INTRIGUED WITH the contrast between the cleanliness of the bars' countertops and the mess that accumulates underneath. The more popular the place, the bigger the mess because people throw cigarette butts, napkins, cupcake and muffin wrappers on the floor at their feet all day long.

In comparison to the United States, this region (at least) of Spain has public bathrooms that are spiffy. Most restrooms are quite clean. Often the floors or walls are of marble; the fixtures are of good quality. And, contrary to stories about the poor quality or lack of toilet paper, they usually have an adequate supply.

Many of the restrooms have lights that are on a timer: a very clever idea in my opinion. *Usually* they stay on ample time to use the facilities, wash hands, and get out. However, once I once got caught short. I had gone into the stall and hit the light switch. The overhead light went on and the timer started. I sat down on the toilet. Ten seconds later the light went out. Luckily, when my eyes adjusted I could see that a tiny light in the switch remained on, so I was not completely in the dark while searching for the toilet paper and doorknob.

JOURNAL, DAY 22, resumes: It is now the middle of the night; the church's chimes just rang one. I'm sitting in the bathroom on the commode so I won't keep Ralph awake while I write this entry. I'm wrapped in a couple of big towels to keep warm; all of our clothing is now freshly washed and is hanging from every conceivable place so it'll dry.

Ralph said not to overdo the e-mails (I guess he's afraid I'll be a pest) so I'm feeling frustrated by not being able to write. If I don't want to write in my journal in the evening, I usually have only one alternative: more walking! That's another reason for the frequent e-mails!

JOURNAL, DAY 23 (Sunday, September 23): León. Layover day.

WE ATE WHAT I consider to be a civilized breakfast, fresh orange juice, tea, and delightful, flaky, fruit-filled pastries, at a bakery near the cathedral.

We made our way to the *Parador San Marcos* and the León Museum, which are both housed in the same beautiful building. They are just a twenty-minute walk from where we are staying in the center of town. Once a monastery, the *San Marcos* is now the best place to stay in León (a five-star hotel). Both the hotel and the museum are impressive in their own way. Across from the parador is a monument to pilgrims. Ralph and I took photos of each other: posing easily as wet and weary pilgrims.

Ralph suggested we stay at the parador overnight, but I don't really have any burning desire to do so. Our hotel room is not terribly fancy, but its skylight adds charm and looks as if it belongs in an artist's garret. In addition, we like being close to everything.

NEXT, WE WALKED to the bus station. We've been discussing for a few days if we can make it to Santiago and back to Madrid in time for our scheduled flight home if we continue on hiking. At the hotel, I had calculated and re-calculated the mileage ahead of us and the days required, trying to come up with a reasonable itinerary so that we could continue on foot. Neither of us wants to give up on our original plan of walking the entire 500 miles.

At the bus station, we sat on the hard benches in the massive waiting room, rehashing and reevaluating the pros and cons of walking vs. riding. There are several bona-fide reasons for taking the bus. First, we know that although it might be possible to make it to Santiago time-wise, we'd be under a lot of pressure to do many high-mileage days and that's definitely contrary to the spirit of the trail. Second, it's only been eleven days since 9/11, and we don't know for certain if our flight is still scheduled. Finally, we both have colds and the weather forecast is for continued rain.

Taking the bus will save us several days of walking. We agreed that it was better to miss the next hundred miles by taking the bus to Ponferrada than to have to bus the last one hundred miles into Santiago. I am sorry that we'll miss seeing the next towns. We'd looked forward to seeing Hospital de Orbigo and Astorga in particular, but I have to agree this is the best decision, all things considered. I still find it depressing and feel that I've failed at something.

We went to the refugio to have our certificate stamped. There was Malu, just arrived. We had a happy reunion, then a tearful goodbye, when we explained that we were going to bus ahead and would not be able to finish with her.

The refugio host translated Malu's Portuguese for us. "I find it is touching how Ralph and you care for each other; he tending your feet," she said. "I wish I spoke English, and that you would visit Brazil," she continued.

WE WENT TO lunch together. It was a workout to talk to her (and vice-versa), but we were all determined to keep trying to understand each other. We learned that she also has recently retired from teaching (though she taught high school, whereas I taught elementary). Tears flowed again as we hugged and departed.

Later, when we were walking toward the Cathedral, we ran into Rosanna. We had to tell her goodbye also. We learned that she still was staying in the refugios and traveling by herself.

"I don't go very fast; hurrying seems to be opposite of the lesson of the trail," she said.

"We miss some things about the refugios, but we needed a good night's sleep," I said. "Besides, Ralph has a cold, and he'd be keeping everyone awake with his coughing."

"That's not a problem," Rosanna answered, "you can't help that, but it's different in the refugios now, people don't even try to be quiet."

It reminded me how much the quality of one's experience of the Camino is dependent on the people one chances to meet along its route.

Ralph and I continued down the avenue to the cathedral. Spectacular! Totally unreal! How aptly its nickname describes it, "The Cathedral without Walls." Where one might expect stone walls, there are gloriously colorful stained glass windows. If ever I have experienced being bowled over, this was it.

Seeing it brought a flood of questions to my mind, "Who can conceive of such a thing?" "Design it?" "How many people does it take to build it?" "How long did it take?"

I remembered a scene from yesterday. We were hiking along and I happened to notice a house that looked just like the ones I used to draw in kindergarten—just like *every* kid probably draws in elementary school. The house was rectangular in shape, with two windows in front, and a door. It was built of bricks and had a front walk leading straight to the front door. There was a tree on one side. There was smoke curling out of the chimney. "I could build that," I thought.

THEN, TODAY, WE see the cathedral and stand before it in awe at what amazing things the human mind can imagine and create. The inside of the cathedral is equally impressive. Sunlight shines through the multitude of colorful transparent panes portraying craftsmen at work, donors next to saints, and religious themes. High up on the walls are carvings depicting the happenings of Hell; themes of "fire and brimstone" come to mind. We studied the carvings of the choir stalls—the floors, walls, and seats covered with the meticulous, intricate work of several sculptors over the course of many years during the mid-1400s—until we could absorb no more.

Our two hours at the cathedral spent examining the fine details of the art within and the broader scope of the exterior were far too few. For some, a lifetime of study of this beautiful Gothic cathedral might not be enough, but for us ordinary folk, a couple of visits on a few different occasions would be time well spent. I understood why some of the guidebooks recommended bringing binoculars in order to see into the farthermost corners.

WE LATER LEARNED that the present cathedral is the fourth church on this site. Construction was begun in 1205 and essentially completed in 1302. For work of this magnitude, one hundred years is considered a short time. The project progressed rapidly because of its solid financial and political support. There have been several additions and modifications, primarily made in the 1400s and 1500s.

JOURNAL RESUMES: AT eight-thirty tomorrow morning, we are going to catch a bus at the station and take it for about one hundred miles to Ponferrada. Unfortunately we are going to miss seeing many places which we would have found interesting. First is a small town, La Virgen del Camino. It does not have a refuge, but does have both hostel and restaurants. The modern church is believed to be the site of the following miracle:

The Legend of La Virgen del Camino

In the early sixteenth century, the Virgin Mary appeared to a local shepherd and demanded that he build her a shrine. The bishop of León was unconvinced until the shepherd used his slingshot to hurl a pebble that turned into a boulder on striking the ground. The cult of the Virgin took off rapidly, spreading throughout León in a few short years. In 1522, a merchant was held captive, chained inside a strongbox, by the Moors in North Africa. The Virgin, knowing of the merchant's desire to visit her shrine, miraculously transported him, chain, box, and all, to La Virgen del Camino.

"The facade of the modern 1961 church is dominated by a massive, modernist sculpture of the Virgin and the Apostles, with Santiago pointing toward Compostela. Inside, the merchant's box and chains are held in the sacristy. The Virgen del Camino's feast days are on Sep. 15 and Oct. 10."

(version from Davies and Cole, pg. 125)

Although we didn't hike it, here is what we had been look-ing forward to: after Virgen del Camino, the Camino route again splits, for a short distance. One route is the more traditional, but is alongside the highway. The other is about more than a mile longer, but more scenic and quiet.

The routes converge at the small town of Hospital de Orbigo. This town, on the bank of the River Orbigo, has been the scene of many battles and many floods. Yet the multi-arched Gothic bridge has always been rebuilt in its original style. Some scholars believe that an event that took place on the bridge, the tournament of Don Suero de Qui-nones, may have been the inspiration for Cervantes' book *Don Quixote*.

Don Suero de Quinones

In 1434, or thereabouts, a young man named Don Suero de Quinones was rejected by the woman he loved. Tormented by his love for her, he decided to put an iron collar around his neck to symbolize that he was still attached to her. He promised to wear the collar until he had broken the lances of 300 of Europe's best knights on the bridge at Orbigo.

During the holy year, in the two-week period preceding Dia de Santiago (July 25), Suero and his friends successfully fought off all comers. When the competition was finished, Suero took the collar from his neck, collected a jeweled bracelet from his lady-fair and took it to Santiago de Compostela. Today, visitors can view the bracelet in the cathedral's museum; it encircles the neck of the statue of Santiago Alfeo. Each year, in early June, this famous tournament is re-enacted next to the Gothic bridge of Hospital de Orbigo.

(adapted from Davies and Cole, pg. 126

NOT BEING ON foot and able to visit the city of Astorga and its surrounding region was a great disappointment.

We missed seeing Antonio Gaudi's *Palacio Episcopal*. This palace was begun in 1889 for Archbishop Juan Bautista

Grau Vallespinos, but he never lived in it. For him it was too extravagant; he condemned it for its "fanciful, whimsical architecture." It was used by Franco's party during the Spanish Civil War, then became the home of the *Museo de los Caminos*, with its collection of statues and art of St. James. Nearby are the cathedral and the *Museo Diocesano*, both of which are worth a visit.

One of the unusual features of the Astorga area is that it's home to a group of people known as the Maragatos. Their origins are debated among scholars. Some assert that the Maragatos are related to the Berbers, some say to the Phoenicians, still others believe they are descendents of slaves brought north by the Moors. For centuries they were muleteers, using the beasts of burden to haul heavy loads from Spain's north coast into the interior.

Traditionally the Maragatos kept to themselves. They limited contact with outsiders, did not welcome them to their celebrations, and did not allow inter-marriage. Nowadays they are increasingly being assimilated into the dominant culture and little of their unique culture remains. At Astorga's *Plaza de Espana*, visitors can view traditionally-dressed Maragatos figurines striking the bell of the town hall each hour. One figurine is of Pero Mato, the Maragatos folk hero who fought alongside Santiago at the Battle of Clavijo.

While in the Astorga region, visitors can partake of a hearty traditional meal known as *Cocido Maragato*. This lunchtime meal begins with a substantial dish of ham, chicken, pork, venison ear, and other meats with hair and skin still attached. Following the meat dishes are vegetables, soup, and finally dessert. After this feast will come famine unless you pack some food for the miles through the mountains that lie ahead.

Villafranca del Bierzo in the foothills of the Cantabrians.

REGION 4

THE CANTABRIAN RANGE

Region 4 – The Cantabrian Range

- Astorga to Rabanal del Camino   13 miles
- Rabanal del Camino to El Acebo   10.5 miles
- El Acebo to Ponferrada   10 miles
- Ponferrada to Santiago   125 miles
- Ponferrada to Cacabelos   9.5 miles
- Cacabelos to Trabadelo   12 miles

Knights Templar castle in Ponferrada.

11 • Astorga to Trabadelo

Of the Maragatos, El Bierzo, and the Fairy-tale Castle

Why do strong arms fatigue themselves with frivolous dumbbells? To dig a vineyard is worthier exercise for men.
—Marcus Valerius Martialis (40 CE – 103 CE)

Approximately fifty miles from León and just after Astorga, the trail leaves the meseta and enters a mountainous region. One soon passes near the village of Valdeviejas. At its far side, the main route leads to the village of Murias de Rechivaldo, which has a refugio (open all year).

A second route, only slightly longer, goes through Castrillo de los Polvazares. Though the old ways are dying out, this wonderfully-restored village will give you a glimpse of the traditional Maragatos homes with their walls of stone and slate roofs. My recommendation is to visit both, which involves only a slight detour on the way to Rabanal del Camino.

Another ten miles along the Camino is the hamlet of Rabanal del Camino. It is a traditional stop; it was the ninth one listed in the *Codex Calixtinus*. Soon after, one begins a climb on alternately dirt trail and paved road through countryside covered with heather and gorse. Wolves, though seldom spotted, live in the area. Ahead is the nearly abandoned village of Foncebadón, a tantalizing hamlet. It's an interesting place for photographers with its cluster of deserted homes, its piles of collapsed buildings, its worn cobblestone streets, and its omnipresent rain or snow. As you continue your uphill hike, stop for a final view.

In less than a mile, you'll come to *Cruz de Fierro* (Cross of Fire) at the pass over Monte Irago (4,933 ft./1504 m.). Cruz de Fierro is a huge pile of rocks at the pass over Monte Irago that is also the border between the regions of La Maragateria and El Bierzo. It's been an important stop for pilgrims for centuries. The tradition of placing a stone at high points along one's journey is an old one, a way to appease the gods and to insure a safe journey through the treacherous mountains. (It is much like the travelers' custom in Hawaii of placing a stone on the side of the trail, sometimes wrapped in a ti leaf, as an offering to the demigod Kamapuala for luck and safety on the journey.)

At Cruz de Fierro, present day pilgrims still place a stone for good luck. Many have brought one from home for this purpose; others pick one up along the way. Some write their name and the date of their visit, others leave a message for friends or a prayer to their god. There's also a cross atop the Cruz de Fierro and a shelter (both more recent additions).

After descending on a paved road for a mile or two, travelers reach the hamlet of Manjarín. There you will find one of the most interesting refugio hosts on the Camino, Tomás. Tomás, in fact, is the *only* resident of the town. Apparently his is not the spiffiest refugio along the Camino, but Tomás makes up for that by his hospitality and his stories. In the morning, he rings a bell that hangs outside to bring luck to departing pilgrims. A couple of miles further on is the highest point on the Camino—almost 5,000 feet.

As travelers cross through the valleys and pass through the villages of El Acebo and Riego de Ambrós, they increasingly see the beautiful slate roofs and stone homes that dominate this area. After leaving El Acebo, the trail passes a monument to Heinrich Krause, a cyclist en route to Santiago who died here after being hit by a car in 1987.

The next small town is Molinaseca. It sits next to a large river and its bridges provided strategic points of control during Roman and medieval times. Its beautiful setting also drew members of the aristocracy; many of their fine homes are still standing.

Those taking the most direct route will soon enter Ponferrada. Those wanting a more interesting (but longer) route into Ponferrada will take a slight jog to Campo, which was Ponferrada's Jewish district during medieval times. Follow the sign to *Iglesia Silo XVII*. This route leads through a neighborhood of wonderfully restored slate and stone houses.

Because we took the bus the one hundred miles from León to Ponferrada, we quickly entered a new region, mountains of the Cantabrian range. Its climate and terrain are a dramatic contrast to the meseta now behind us. Ponferrada's location at 1,781 feet elevation, in a valley formed by the Sil River, is more protected from harsh winter weather than the mountain passes that lie ahead.

Ponferrada, now a city of 60,000, took its name from its former bridge (*pons* translates to bridge; *ferrada* to iron). On one side of the river is the picturesque old city, on the other is the modern, industrial area. Until the mid-1900s coal mining was an important industry in Ponferrada; now one sees huge slagheaps on the outskirts of town.

JOURNAL, DAY 24 (Monday, September 24): **León to Ponferrada via bus; hike Ponferrada to Cacabelos (9.5 miles/15 km).**

AFTER ARRIVING MID-MORNING at the bus station in Ponferrada we asked directions to the center of town. Then, we started off to find the city's medieval castle: a Knights Templar castle built in the 13th century. It was the stronghold of the Knights to protect pilgrims traveling through the area and was one of the largest fortresses in northwestern Spain.

Ponferrada is a large city, and we did not have a local map. We asked a man approaching us on the street for directions to the castle. He began to explain. As usual, we understood about the first three words, but we kept nodding our heads in agreement. He was not so easily fooled.

He smiled. "No, you *don't* understand," he said. He gestured for us to follow him, which we did.

A couple of blocks further, he stopped again. He tried again to explain which way to go. We tried to indicate we understood, even though we didn't, so that we could let him off the hook. But, he still didn't buy it. He insisted on escorting us a little further in the right direction. Only when he was assured that he had taken us far enough that we could get there the rest of our way on our own did he shake hands goodbye and send us on our way. I often wonder if Americans in general are as kind to visitors as Ralph and I are always treated in other countries.

Usually we find places by what Ralph calls the "binary search." We ask once, get started in the right direction, get a little closer and ask again. Usually by the third time, we are there.

The castle at Ponferrada is the castle of everyone's fantasies—complete with turrets, a moat, and an iron gate. Even though it is a good thirty-minute walk away from the Camino, it's well worth the effort. It was disappointing to find that the castle was closed on Mondays, but simply seeing the exterior was enough to satisfy us.

I enjoyed considering the defense of castles as explained by Gitlitz and Davidson (pg. 289). "Like the entrances to many castles, it is a double gate. Attackers had to bridge the moat, fight through the barbican (the iron grill lowered to block the door), dodge the arrows from the bowmen in the two flanking towers, turn to the right (which put them at a disadvantage, most swordsmen being right-handed), and then breach a second defensive gate before—if they were lucky enough to still be alive and in fighting condition—confronting the massed troops waiting for them on the open ground."

JOURNAL, DAY 24, resumes: We ate a simple lunch at an outdoor café near the castle and then found our own way back to the Camino. In the small town of Compostilla, we stopped briefly to take a photo of a church wall mural honoring the levitating Santa María. And in the next town, Columbrianos, we photographed a mural of St. James, which had been painted on a church wall.

Our hike was pleasant. The skies were blue with scattered clouds. We passed vineyards with both red and green grapes, tremendously large squash, and lots of produce similar to that grown in our region of California. It reminded me of how familiar California must have seemed to the Spanish who settled there.

We stopped at *Prada de Tope,* a busy tourist attraction where wines and other regional foodstuffs are sold and sent around the world. Through an open door we watched the workers preparing and canning peppers. We'd read in our guidebook that pilgrims are offered a free drink and a tapa—carrying on the tradition of helping pilgrims—after 5:00 PM. We'd hoped to be welcomed and given some refreshments, but neither happened. I guess this is just another indication that the increasing number of pilgrims is stressing the network.

JOURNAL, DAY 23, resumes: I was still feeling disappointed about missing portions of the trail and giving up on part of our goal by taking the bus for a while. Missing out on a warm welcome at the winery compounded my sense of loss, but I know that the four-hundred miles we will do is not a lightweight achievement, so I'm trying to keep everything in perspective.

WE CHECKED INTO the *Santa María* hostel here in Cacabelos and then turned around and went for a walk through town. We noticed a dump truck backed up to what looked like an ordinary garage. On closer inspection, we saw that the driver was dumping grapes onto the concrete floor of the building. Around the edges of the room was a twelve-inch high concrete barrier creating a reservoir for a floor full of green and purple grapes. Two men wearing knee-high rubber boots stood in the midst of bunches of grapes stomping the fruit. A fourth man stood to the side, shoveling and tossing un-crushed bunches to the middle of the room. There was a drain at the back of the room to catch and collect the juice. I hoped the boots were not the same ones they had worn in the pasture!

JOURNAL, DAY 25 (Tuesday, September 25): Cacabelos to Trabadelo (12 miles/19 km).

THIS WAS A short day; we walked only from eight in the morning until two in the afternoon. Huge clouds provided a beautiful sunrise at the start of the day. Dark, gray clouds covered the sky many times during the day, but we had no rain. I hope it holds to the pattern of rain only in the late afternoon or night. Raining *after* we arrive at our destination is just fine with me!

After we left Cacabelos this morning, we descended to the fertile El Bierzo valley with a temperate microclimate suitable for growing vegetables, tobacco, and, increasingly, wine grapes. Because of the quality of the wines of the region, in particular that made from the Mencia grapes, Bierzo is a *Denominacion de Origen*. The Mencia grape, which is capable of producing fruity red wines, thrives in the well-drained soil of slate and granite.

WE PASSED THROUGH Villafranca del Bierzo, which is a very attractive and popular stopover for pilgrims. It has many structures remaining from medieval times, and it's the last town before the steep climb into the mountains of Galicia. Villafranca del Bierzo has three refugios; the most interesting one has to be the one run by D. Jesús Jato and his family who are dedicated to helping pilgrims. *Ave Fenix,* so nicknamed by Jesus because it has been destroyed by fire and rebuilt, is not a conventional refugio. Some pilgrims complain about the conditions: citing a lack of sanitation and comfort. Others remind themselves that they should appreciate any amenities. There's a sign that hangs in the refugio's bathroom that reads, "the tourist demands, the travelling one is thankful."

But Ave Fenix, besides a bed, a shower, and a communal kitchen, provides healing. Those who are there for the *queimada* will long remember the unique experience. The *queimada* is an alcoholic concoction. The ceremony is also called "the forest fire" because the server puts fire in the drink, which burns in a blue flame because of the drink's alcoholic content.

Traditionally, a shell is used to scoop the liquid out of a vessel, and a cupful is served to each of the participants. Not all of the drink is consumed; a bit, like the starter for sourdough bread, has to be kept to be added to the next *queimada.* Meanwhile, tales are told, spells incanted, and prayers spoken. Those who drink of the forest fire are said to be protected from various ominous entities, such as the witches, the demons, and the bad spirits that one might otherwise encounter while on the Camino.

THERE ARE THREE routes coming out of Villafranca del Bierzo. One is along the shoulder of the freeway; two go into the mountains. The highway route was described as unpleasant and as the most dangerous stretch of the Camino—not much to recommend that. (The 2005 edition of the *Pilgrim*

Guide states that the highway is now much safer because the new freeway has reduced the traffic on the old highway.) We chose the lower of the two mountain routes. Though it added mileage and time to the hike, it turned out to be a lovely walk.

JOURNAL, DAY 25, resumes: The initial climb out of the village was quite steep. It was so damp and humid that sweat soon covered my face and poured from my body, soaking my clothes. But it was one of the most scenic and beautiful days on the Camino; the sun was shining, and everything around us was green. We passed beautiful 100-year-old chestnut trees, wild heather, broom, and pine.

The pines were the first woods we'd seen that didn't look like a tree plantation; they weren't planted in rows. When we looked deep into the valley, we were extremely glad that we had picked the route we had. The highway project below has caused massive degradation of the land.

Trabadelo is similar to the vast majority of formerly Roman towns we've passed through: one long main street with only a few dozen homes and other buildings lining either side. The houses are of plaster or decorated with marble slabs. A few of the smaller homes have roofs covered with moss and grasses. Some of the older homes have thatched roofs, but these are becoming increasingly rare. The craft of thatch-making is dying out, and most homeowners re-roof with more long-lasting slate. The district is known for its slate, and that is what most homeowners now use for roofing. It's placed, not in overlapping rows, but in irregular patterns. (Slate is so costly where we live that it amazes us that there is an area where it is commonplace.)

Trabadelo's major employer is the lumber mill; a few people keep bees. On our stroll through town we found only two bars, and our hostel, the *Hostal Nova Ruta*; there is no refugio. As I considered the accommodations, I was once again pleased that our room was inexpensive, clean and pleasant (as most hostels have been). I'd much rather stay in these basic rooms than in any of the U.S. budget motels that glue the lamps to their fake wood tables and dressers.

THIS REGION SEEMS less well-off than most; many people are engaged in subsistence farming. However, what they may lack in income, they gain in quality food. The produce is fresh. Pails of potatoes, cabbage, or onions sit out front of several homes. If you want produce, you knock and wait for someone to come to the door and take your coins in exchange. And when a housewife wants chard for soup, she has only to venture into the garden and pick a few leaves.

In an interesting combination of old and new methods, we saw a threesome preparing peppers: the man with a blowtorch roasting the outside of the peppers, the two women peeling them by hand.

Region 5 – Galicia

- Trabadelo to O Cebreiro   11 miles
- O Cebreiro to Triacastela   13.5 miles
- Triacastela to Sarria   11.5 mile
- Sarria to Santiago   70 miles
- Sarria to Portomarín   14.5 miles
- Portomarín to Palas de Rei   15 miles
- Palas de Rei to Melide   9.5 miles
- Melide to Arzua   9 miles
- Arzua to A Rúa   11.5 miles
- A Rúa to Santiago   12.5 miles

Slate fences in Galicia.

REGION 5

GALICIA

Early morning in Galicia.

Galician late afternoon.

12 • Trabadelo to Portomarín

Into Green Galicia

May the road rise to meet you. May the wind always be at your back. May the sun shine warm upon your face, the rains fall soft upon your fields and, until we meet again, may God hold you in the palm of his hand.

—Irish blessing

Galicia, the last section on the Camino, is quite green with lush vegetation. Because the Atlantic Ocean moderates the weather here, Spaniards and other tourists often head to this coastal area to escape the heat of the interior. But since the lushness is a result of the frequent precipitation, be prepared for mist and rain any time of year.

JOURNAL, DAY 26 (Wednesday, September 26): **Trabadelo to O Cebreiro (11 miles/17.5 km).**

THIS WAS A lovely day. The hike was described in our guidebook as including a steep climb, and to allow at least three hours for that portion. But we didn't find it particularly difficult (thank goodness for all the Sierra hiking!), and enjoyed being surrounded by *green*. And we were surprised, and delighted, to see crocus blooming this time of year; it's a spring-blooming flower in California.

At the start of today's hike, we were on the shoulder of the busy highway, but after a couple of miles, at La Portola, we came to an area where a section of new freeway has been completed. Most of the traffic went that way, leaving our route lightly traveled. Soon we were back on dirt trails, and climbing again. The views were spectacular looking back down the valley and across to several ranges of mountains.

Farmers, wearing their sturdy rubber boots, were busily collecting potatoes far up the mountainside. Ralph and I had to huff and puff to get up here, while the locals, who have spent their lives making this daily climb to work in these steeply-placed farms, probably think nothing of it. Judging once again from the neat rows, weeded plots, and healthy plants, the gardens and farms are a great source of pride.

We are staying in O Cebreiro at *Mesón Anton*, which has a very cute bar, restaurant, and owner.

The tiny village has several houses of Celtic origin. These *pallozas* are well-suited to their ridgetop locations. The buildings are oval, with low stone walls, and with thatched roofs securely attached to wooden poles. Homes have no chimneys; instead the smoke is allowed to escape through the thatched roof. While doing so, the smoke cures the meats hung from the rafters inside. One of the pallozas was open for viewing; others have been left in various stages of completion to show how they're constructed. In addition, the village has several of the region's typical slate-roofed, stone houses.

O Cebreiro has become a tourist destination; many visit here and then set out for Santiago. During the summer, huge tour buses overwhelm the village. Its picturesque setting and buildings make it a favorite stop of pilgrims as well. It's at the highest point in the area, and the 360-degree view from the pass is spectacular.

JOURNAL, DAY 26, resumes: Most of the people we met today

were with walking groups. They are "slackpacking," having their luggage, and sometimes themselves, driven to their overnight accommodations.

Our dinner was also at *Meson Antón*. We ordered *el menú*, but instead of the usual several choices, it was a set menu. First, we were served a salad of flavorful, bright red tomatoes, with onions. Next came the plate with the specialty of the house: *pulpo* (octopus). Ralph and I looked at each other. "Can you eat some of this?" I asked.

"No," replied Ralph. And I somehow convinced him to be the one to tell the poor owner that we didn't care for it. Colorful as it was, and delicious as it might have been, we couldn't bring ourselves to try it. I felt guilty, as I know it's impolite not to try a food served.

Luckily the owner did not treat us like ingrates, but proceeded to serve us the rest of the meal: ham (*real* ham, not deli-sliced) accompanied by tasty, chewy bread and vino tinto. Locally produced goat cheese was our treat for dessert. There's a lot to be said for fresh-from-the-farm food.

Maybe the best part of today's hike was that we could take our time; we don't feel rushed anymore.

LATER IN THE trip we saw that pulpo is very popular in Galicia and is often found on the menu. A traditional *pulperia* will serve the spiced octopus, soaked in wine, on wooden platters accompanied by bread and Ribeiro (a white wine).

JOURNAL, DAY 27 (Thursday, September 27): **O Cebreiro to Triacastela (13.5 miles/21.5 km).**

THOUGH WE REGRET having to bus, and perhaps didn't need to, we're now finding we can walk at a leisurely pace and don't need to hurry. We're still doing about 12 miles a day, but the pressure is off. The countryside is beautiful and justifies a slow passage. It reminds me of springtime in the San Francisco Bay Area: new fronds on the ferns, blossoms on the heather, grazing cows (and many cow pies), and beautiful trees (chestnuts rather than bay). It's hard to believe it is fall.

Galicia is known for its rain, but we've been experiencing beautiful blue skies. After this morning's chill wore off, I was comfortable wearing a tee-shirt and shorts. My bunions didn't start hurting until just about the time we had planned to stop. Most of the time we were going downhill from O Cebreiro's 4,242-foot saddle (the drop to Triacastela is 2,198 feet). The exception was a steep but short uphill at *Alto San Roque* (4,146 feet). The pass is marked by a dramatic pilgrim sculpture.

Our route was along lanes lined by invasive broom and gorse, but also crocus, foxglove, roses (now with rose hips), ferns, and mosses. We were often shaded by oak, chestnut, and pines. We saw numerous piles of what we think was wolf scat. We know they are found here—though rarely seen.

We see a lot of cows and often share a path with them when they are being taken to the fields. It's generally the woman of the household who is carrying a switch and transferring the cows from barn to field. Passing a herd of cows can be tricky. Not only do we have to watch where we step, we also have to avoid being brushed by them. At one point today I had to leap behind a stone slab because I didn't care to get smeared with the muck that covers their rumps. Too much green grass in their diet perhaps? It is, however, pleasant to see them grazing in rich, green pastures rather than standing atop dirt and manure piles on feed lots. The men are busy in the fields: repairing equipment, plowing, harvesting, and such.

JOURNAL, DAY 27, resumes: Two opportunities were presented today that we missed out on. Afterwards, I could have kicked myself for losing sight (again) of "living in the moment." In one of the villages, we passed an old woman sitting in front of her house cooking and selling crepes warm from the pan. In another village, we saw a table covered with small baskets of berries.

"Vine-ripened raspberries" read the hand-painted sign. I love raspberries! In both cases we just walked by because it wasn't mealtime and we had miles to go before day's end.

We're now seeing a completely different set of people as we hike. Most are part of a large tour group (from England) that started in O Cebreiro yesterday. We also are playing leapfrog with an older couple from Australia. They are on their honeymoon, but they're doing the Camino the hard way: walking and carrying everything.

Because we're no longer feeling pressured to hurry, we lingered over lunch today, and stopped often for photos.

WE'RE NOW IN Triacastela. It draws its name from the fact that it had three castles at one time, though it no longer has any. There are five banks, a bar with a computer linked to the Internet, and a market with a sign reading "Supermercado." Although in reality the market is not very big, it does have the first shopping carts we've seen in many weeks.

JOURNAL RESUMES: OUR hostel isn't very fancy; it's one of several large-scale, plain-faced apartment buildings along the highway that runs through town. It does have a row of large windows across one wall where we can look across at hills covered with chestnut trees.

As usual, as soon as we arrived, we showered and washed our clothes. Washing our clothes on such a humid day is probably a waste of time, but we figured that getting our clothes hung up to dry right away gives us the best chance that they will be ready by morning. It's rare now that everything dries overnight, so most mornings we hang the damp clothes from short rope pieces strung across the back of our packs.

I've now lost one pair of underpants, one pair of long underwear bottoms (no great loss, indeed, an opportunity to get a new pair), and the free airline socks that I'd enjoyed padding around in at night. That leaves me with only two pair of underpants; luckily *they* dry fast.

THE AVAILABILITY OF laundry facilities, or at least clotheslines, is one advantage of staying in refugios. When we began staying in small hotels, it became more difficult to get our clothes washed and dried. We ended up hanging our wet laundry from curtain rods, window fasteners, radiators, shower curtain rods—anywhere we could find that would not be damaged by the dripping clothes.

The rooms always have radiators, but none are operational yet (management appears to be waiting for even nippier nights). So with the marble floors and increasingly chilly temperatures, we are now looking for extra blankets at night. Such a contrast to the beginning of the trip when I would wake up in the middle of the night in a sweat.

Because today was such a lovely, enjoyable day, and we are relatively close to done (about eighty miles to go), I'm beginning to feel that I don't want our trip it to end. We visited Triacastela's *Church of Santiago* where we found a copy of the following poem written by the parish priest, August Losada Lopez:

Don't Give Up!

When things are going badly, as sometimes happens,
When the path appears uphill,
When your resources are weakened and doubts emerge,
When, smiling, you have to choke back the tears,
When worries weigh you down,
Rest, if you need to, but don't give up.
Life is strange with its comings and goings,
Where contradictions are our daily bread.
So if defeat comes knocking on your door
and invites you to be backward-looking, do not let it in.
Fight it off. Keep looking to the future, don't give in.
Triumph may be just around the corner.
Triumph is defeat in reverse.
It is the silver lining in every cloud
Which never lets you see just how near it is,

Even when you have it a hand's grasp away.
That's why you must decide to fight without respite,
Because in truth,
when the going gets tough the tough get going.

In the hope that the journey of life and Santiago not
be a burden to you, but rather a meeting with Jesus the
pilgrim and with Jesus of Nazareth, to see what we can
contribute to making this world a better place spiritually
and humanly. You have the world in your hands. Your
fellow man's happiness depends on you. May the peace
and love of Jesus be with you!

L eaving Triacastela, pilgrims have a choice of two routes
to Sarria. Our route took us directly to Sarria. Though
it's the original route, it is now partly paved. It's also about
five miles shorter than the alternate. The alternate route
goes through Samos. Most pilgrims who go through Samos
make this detour in order to visit its famous Benedictine
monastery. Visitors can take a thirty-minute guided tour of
the enormous facility. Pilgrims can stay in the monastery's
refugio or one of the town's hostels. Though there are several good places to eat in Samos, there is only one bar along
the route between Triacastela and Samos (almost 7 miles)
and one between Samos and Sarria (about 10 miles).

JOURNAL, DAY 28 (Friday, September 28): **Triacastela to Sarria
(11.5 miles/18.5 km).**

WE TOOK THE shorter of the two routes to get here. We passed
through several very small villages: A Balsa, San Xil, Furela, and
Calvor. We did find a couple of worthy spots to visit: a Romanesque church with a beautiful chandelier, and the ruins of
a 12th-century castle.
     We stopped in the village of Furela for a snack. The only place
we could find food for sale was at a small, uninviting shop. We

ordered sodas. A young man pushed the cans through a small window of the kiosk. I was reminded of the Plexiglas shields surrounding some of the cashiers at gas stations and the bank tellers back home. We ate our picnic lunch (the usual salami and cheese on a roll) with our sodas.

DURING TODAY'S HIKE we were often following country lanes: uneven rocky trails lined with six to ten-foot high walls of crumbling stone covered with mosses and ferns. Oak trees, with their heavy branches, created dark tunnels. The dark forests conjured up images of sprites and fairies. It's beginning to look like fall; the wind tries to rip the dwindling number of yellow leaves from the birches and poplars. I can't believe that I am saying this, but I am enjoying myself, and feeling somewhat sad that our hiking has to end. I find myself walking more slowly (than usual) so I can savor the experience and the land.

We're hearing many songbirds. It seems in great contrast to the earlier sections of the Camino where we saw few birds other than the ubiquitous crows and sparrows. We're not experts on the matter, but I wonder if the way that the earlier forests are managed has something to do with it. "Managed care" often appears to mean that trees are planted in rows and columns and that the lower branches, which would otherwise provide coverage, have been trimmed out. It could also be the time of year. Whatever the reason, it's pleasant to see the variety of birds in this area.

We have seen only two squirrels during our entire trip (at home, we frequently see them in our oak trees). It's curious. There are acorns in great abundance—both in the trees and on the ground—yet we see no oak seedlings.

One of the highlights of today was being on the trail for a while with a young French group. They were singing the traditional children's song *Alouette* as they marched along. It seems a number of people sing to entertain themselves as they are hiking.

Sarria is at a lower elevation than Triacastela was, but that doesn't mean that we spent the day only going downhill. It was a day of up, up, up so that we could descend even more. The weather is changing; it's much more humid. It was on and off with jacket and cap today because of the wind. It's now raining.

We decided, because we miss the community of hikers, to stay in a refugio again. It was lucky for us that we arrived in Sarria early in the afternoon. The guidebook indicated an opening time of six, but when we checked in at two-thirty the place was almost full. Señora asked everyone's age and then opened her last room for those of us who were fifty or older and married. Those who arrived later were allowed to put their sleeping pads on the floor in the hallway. I felt sorry for those who had planned to have a late arrival.

The bathroom is unisex and, to my mind, poorly arranged. There's no place to hang or set clothes in the shower stall. And, you can't step out to dress after showering because there are multiple mirrors placed above the nearby washbasins. Still, we are lucky to have warm beds. The refugio has a washer and dryer, but we decided to wash our clothes by hand since it would have taken forever to wait our turn on the machines.

WE SET OUT to explore the town. We stopped for dinner and ordered el menú. The owner brought a bottle of wine. When he opened it, the neck of the bottle shattered. He decided to decant it to a pitcher, and then into an empty bottle. We decided it was safe to drink, if we were careful. We took small sips through closed teeth instead of large swallows.

Our meal began with a garbanzo bean soup followed by a flat, white fish, and a commercially-prepared flan for dessert. (The soup broth was good, the rest "okay." Why is everything beginning to taste the same?)

We came back to the refugio to find that the Señora was upset; the grate over which we had hung our laundry was open at the bottom and our clothes had been dripping down on people seated at the dinner table below. Oops! This may have been the one time I was lucky not to understand much Spanish. We found the offending laundry in the bathroom in a lump where Señora had dumped it.

JOURNAL, DAY 29 (Saturday, September 29): **Sarria to Porto-marín (14.5 miles/23 km).**

WE'VE BEEN GONE for a month; it seems forever! Last evening's rain was enough to put a damper on wandering around the town. It poured during the night, but though the sky this morning indicated rain, we only had occasional sprinkles. When it stopped completely. I was able to pin my wet socks to my backpack to dry. By the end of the day, I was in shorts again. We're continuing to descend in elevation while trekking through small forested areas and hamlets; the hamlets usually consist of four or five houses.

Today we had an important milestone (or maybe I should say kilometer stone?). We passed the signpost indicating that it is only one hundred kilometers to Santiago. To receive the *Compostela* (the certificate) in Santiago, it is only necessary to walk, bicycle, or ride a horse these last 100 kilometers. Most people, however, do *far* more. From here on in, there will be an official marker every kilometer.

With the exception of the German couple we met back in the Arroyo de San Bol (midway across the meseta), the people we now see daily are a new group of fellow travelers. We don't know anyone's name (primarily because we are not staying in the refuges often), but it's still fun to encounter the same people several times a day.

We continue to have our credential stamped each day, and we are starting to think about what we'll say at the pilgrims' office when we are asked the reason for our pilgrimage. The authors of one guidebook describe a lengthy interview process before being granted the *Compostela* because the certificate is not to be given for such frivolous reasons as wanting to have a vacation.

It wouldn't be honorable to say we've done it for religious reasons, but we've decided that saying it was for spiritual reasons is appropriate. Ralph has defined that as wanting to find a sense of presence of those who have traveled the path before, and feeling inspired by meeting so many young people who're seeking answers for their lives by making the pilgrimage. I've defined spiritual as wanting to have time to contemplate my direction as I face a major life change: retirement.

I also believe that walking across a country is the best way to see it and to have it "stay with you." I like driving and sightseeing trips, too, but it's a more limited experience of a place than long-distance walking is. When driving, the sense of a place primarily comes from what we *see*. On foot, we experience our surroundings in several ways. We instantly *feel* the change in temperature when a cloud moves across the face of the sun. We *hear* the dry sunflowers start to rustle as the tiny zephyrs of wind move through. We *see* a blue heron, startled by our sudden appearance, take flight over the watercourse. We *smell* the fragrance of the purple heather.

I've enjoyed sections of the Camino that I probably wouldn't have noticed if we'd just driven through. The meseta, for example, with its straight track, rows of trees, and shimmering heat waves is cemented into my memory because I experienced it for several days. If we had driven through it in one day, the images would have quickly been covered over by the splendors of the major cities such as Burgos and León.

JOURNAL RESUMES: THOUGH there are some hostels and a refugio here in Portomarín, we decided to stay at the three-star *Pousada de Portomarín*. The hotel is very new, with beautiful rooms, yet nearly empty. Our room is very comfortable; it's furnished with upholstered chairs, a table, and a mini-bar. The hotel was built to accommodate tourists after the new city was built. (The hotel initially failed, but reopened in 1998.)

We were the also the only guests in the dining room for dinner—and we had a delicious soup and fish. Though this is the off-season, we suspect that Portomarín is not enjoying the relative prosperity it had during the height of the pilgrimage.

PORTOMARÍN IS A mid-sized town. One of the more noticeable things about it is that the bridge that enters the city from the east is high above the river. Far below are what remain of the previous bridge and many old buildings. At one time, all these structures were underwater, flooded when a dam (the *Embalse de Belesar*) was built downstream. But before construction of the dam was begun in 1956, the church of St. Nicolas, and several other important buildings, were carefully dismantled stone by stone and moved to higher ground, where they still stand. The remains of the old city have gradually become exposed as the water has been drained.

In earlier times, Portomarín was a wealthy town. When Laffi wrote of it, he described it as being divided "by a large river with plenty of fish, particularly eels and excellent trout, which provide us with a magnificent supper."

13 • Portomarín to A Rúa/Arca

We're Coasting Home
… if you want the rainbow, you gotta put up with the rain.
—Dolly Parton

JOURNAL, DAY 30 (Sunday, September 30): **Portomarín to Palas de Rei (15 miles/24.5 km).**

THE HOTEL PROVIDED a generous breakfast buffet including pastries, fruits, and corn flakes, but not Cheerios, which I find myself craving. Most of today's hike was downhill. The rain is still holding off. We still see cattle along the way.

We've encountered a new mystery, part of the manmade landscape: small structures, but substantially built. Some are of stone; some are built with the open, red cement blocks often used in construction here. These outbuildings are about four feet by fifteen feet. On the narrower end, some of the buildings have ornate doors; often the structures are decorated with a family name, a cross, or metal scrollwork.

We wondered if they were private family chapels, but realized the structures weren't wide enough for that. We finally asked. They are *horreos:* raised outbuildings for the storage of corn (which we would call corncribs) while protecting the crop from moisture and rodents. We saw a lot of these as we continued through Galicia.

Until today we hadn't seen anyone washing clothes out-of-doors. We've encountered washtubs with a built-in corrugated ramp for rubbing and scrubbing of clothes. This afternoon, however, we noticed a woman doing her laundry in a river. Because of the prevalence of clotheslines, we've determined that most people don't have dryers. Hotels perhaps.

Palas de Rei is a mid-sized town combining old and new; we saw cows walking down the sidewalk passing right next to a stucco building that housed an Internet site. Our hostel is clean and newly-painted.

While eating dinner at our hotel, Ralph noticed a familiar figure, "Is that Anna at the table behind you?" he asked.

I looked closely, recognized her jacket, and then jumped up to say hello.

"What are you doing here?" she asked. "I've been walking twenty-five to thirty miles a day. It's really tiring, but I was running out of time."

We had to tell the truth, "We felt we had to take the bus to save some time." It was a sweet reunion.

JOURNAL, DAY 31 (Monday, October 1): **Palas de Rei to Melide (9.5 miles/15.5 km).**

THE SKY WAS so dark when we left Palas de Rei, it looked like something from Hemingway's *The Old Man and the Sea.* It was a later start than usual; we didn't get going until 8:30. But as providence would have it, there was Anna on the trail; we walked together for a while.

"I hope I can finish in two more days; I'm ready to be done. I don't see any of the old group, and the refugios don't have the same atmosphere," she said. But since she lives near Santiago, she may well see us in the city when we arrive, which should be Thursday.

THE WALK TODAY was more of the same: dairy, hamlets, and, eventually, heather. Midway, in Leboreiro, we stopped to visit the pretty 13th-century Romanesque Church of Santa María. We found the retablo and wall paintings especially appealing; not all small parish churches are able to maintain their treasured art in such good condition. The priest gave a brief explanation of what we were seeing: "One unique feature of the statue of Christ is that one of his arms is held up, and one is down (unlike most where both arms are upraised); it shows our connection to God, from heaven to earth, is through Him."

We crossed a medieval bridge with four arches as we entered the old village of Furelos. Furelos at one time had a pilgrim hospice; it now has a bar and small restaurant where we stopped for a snack. We kept hearing a car horn honk a few times, stop for a few minutes, and honk again. Finally the car came hurtling into view. The driver braked to a stop in front of a house across the street, hopped out of his car, hung a loaf of bread on the door, and beeped his horn again to alert the residents of their morning delivery.

Soon after Furelos, you are in the suburbs of Melide. During the time of the medieval pilgrimage, Melide (present-day population 8,000) provided important services to travelers. It had four hospices and numerous inns. During our visit, we peeked into a couple of churches. Gitlitz and Davidson note that one of the chapels, the *Ortario de San Antonio,* is almost always open. That makes it quite different from most of the monuments along the Camino; most are usually closed, and you have to content yourself with peeking through a window or keyhole, or hunting down someone with a key.

JOURNAL, DAY 31, resumes: We also visited the *Museo Etnofrafico* (Ethnographic Museum), which had many items from Neolithic times. Of more interest to us were the displays of shoemakers' tools and of the wooden clogs worn by farmers in the field. There were also exhibits of items for school, weaving, carpentry, forging, and clothing of earlier times.

One outfit, obviously to be worn by the Galician farmers in horrendously inclement weather, was made entirely of straw, but there was no explanation to tell us if such garments are still in use and if they were worn locally.

I ANSWERED E-MAILS. We used up an hour looking for an Internet place and answering the messages. News from home awaited us. Life in the U.S. seems, for most, to be back to normal. Karen and Mike, after flights to Russia were resumed, were able to pick up their baby from the adoption agency.

> Mon, 01 Oct. 2001
> Hi Susan,
>   Sounds awesome. We were also very lucky with the weather in Moscow and St. Petersburg. Home with baby Sarah now—I miss sleep...
>   Karen

JOURNAL, DAY 31, resumes: I arranged another week off from teaching. That'll allow me to recover from jet lag and go through our six weeks' worth of mail before we turn around and fly to Las Vegas for Scott and Anne's wedding on the weekend.

Today was a short day; tomorrow will be even shorter, only fourteen kilometers. It's just the way the accommodations fall at this point. I'm sensing the end of the trip; I'm ready to finish.

Our room here is 3500 pesetas (about $20 U.S.); rooms are less expensive now because we're into October. Our *menú* cost 1,000 pesetas and included chicken pasta soup (with the tureen left at the table for refills), lamb shanks (which were very fatty, but had delicious morsels), wine, bread, and ice cream.

JOURNAL, DAY 32 (Tuesday, October 2): **Melide to Arzua (9 miles/14 km).**

WE HAD READ that churros and chocolate are the traditional breakfast in Spain, so I was pretty excited last night when I spotted a sign in a bar picturing them. We made our way through the dark streets early this morning to have some. Imagine my disappointment when we arrived to find no churros or chocolate! We had to start off with day-old croissants and packaged donuts.

Our ever-westward route today took us up a hill, then down to a stream through terrain that slopes towards the south. We walked through a couple of hamlets and passed both pine trees and increasing stands of eucalyptus. Mostly we were on dirt-gravelly roads. We may be slower than some on downhill or flat, but we pass many on the upgrades.

I told Ralph long ago, "I have two speeds, and if you don't like this one, you sure won't like the other (slower) one." We average about two miles an hour.

We saw a couple of bicyclists today. We've seen very few in recent weeks: a big contrast to the many we saw at the start.

When we stopped for lunch, we treated ourselves to *Cerveza Grande* to enjoy with our picnic sandwiches. Afterwards we decided that having beer at lunch is not a good idea. We felt drained of both energy and will. We had to continue walking; what we really wanted to do was take a nap.

In this area, until fairly recently, a family could be recognized as it approached by the unique sound of its particular wooden wheeled, oxen-pulled cart (much like the engine noise of a family car alerts a family dog that his owner is coming home). We saw only one cart today—unfortunately abandoned in favor of more-modern transportation.

JOURNAL RESUMES: TODAY was a short mileage day; we're in Arzua. I liked *Casa Frade* from the moment we arrived. It's a family-owned operation; the proprietor looks as if he's at least 80 years old. The bar is very old-fashioned and behind it are four large, wooden wine barrels. Two are labeled "B" for blanco, and two "T" for tinto. The owner served us the wine in white, ceramic cups about the size of a miniature Chinese rice bowl for forty pesetas (about fifty cents) each. The white wine of the region, Ribeiro, is very smooth and mildly fruity. This region is well known for its cheese, so we asked to sample some. We were served a large plateful of their white cheese with another cup of wine.

Our octogenarian host nodded for us to follow him to our room. His wife looked out from the kitchen when we went past and seemed disappointed when we said we had already eaten lunch. We climbed the stairs and I noticed that, despite his advanced age, our host did not huff and puff.

After we bathed, we washed clothes and hung them on the enclosed balcony. It's useful to have clotheslines strung in a place where it rains nearly every day! Even when it doesn't rain, the humidity has become so high that I'm constantly sweaty and clammy.

ENTICING ODORS DRIFTED from the kitchen teased us through the afternoon. At dinner time, we went downstairs and waited for the menu. Hardly had we been seated when Señora came bustling out of the kitchen, grabbed my hand, and pulled me through the swinging door into the aroma-filled room. Ralph followed right behind me. Senora lifted the lids off of each pot and rattled off our choices: "*Caldo*" (a thick soup), "*Sopa de Macaroni*" (a soup with pasta), or, she pointed to a large bowl of lettuces, we could have *ensalada mixta*.

For our main course, we chose from several huge pots filled with bubbling lamb stew, fricasseed chicken with potatoes and carrots, or boiled potatoes. How to decide which tempting dishes to have? I elected to have the salad and the chicken. For desert, we had a slice of the regional *Torta de Santiago* (a delectable almond cake decorated with a simple sugar-dusted cross of Santiago on top).

"Señora, you are very charming," I managed to say in my limited Spanish. She *was* charming, and obviously she was most happy when she could share her food with appreciative guests. We saw only one other couple at mealtime; I wondered how our host couple managed to stay in business with so few visitors.

...WE HAVE ONLY 23 miles to go!

JOURNAL, DAY 33 (Wednesday, October 3): **Arzua to A Rúa (next door to Arca) (11.5 miles/18.5 km).**

LAST NIGHT'S TV coverage was primarily about flooding in nearby areas. Based on that, we expected to have a nasty, stormy day and encounter muddy trails, but though it was foggy and overcast at first, the sun came out often and the day was quite pleasant. The trail was good, not mucky. In many places it is worn down to bedrock, and it was easy to imagine the feet of countless pilgrims passing through these slate-fenced lanes over the eons of the trail's existence. We passed through many forested sections: eucalyptus, pine, and fir.

During the morning, we saw a group of six people ahead. Four of them had no packs; the other two had only daypacks. As we watched, a car picked up some of them to transport them, or their packs, ahead. "Slack-packing," it's called. Legitimate, unless they claim they walked, which I imagine a certain number do.

Lunch, of regional foods, was good. We had *Caldo Galicia* (a chicken-based soup with chard), fish steaks, and ice cream. The ice cream *looks* like the slabs of Neapolitan ice cream we get at home, but there the similarity ends. The ice cream is actually very rich, like *gelato*.

BECAUSE OF OUR strange experience a couple of days ago—the incident where the waiter simply decanted our wine when the neck of the bottle broke—I held my breath to see what would happen when a fly landed in my soup during lunch today. Fortunately, I didn't have to create a scene; the waitress apologized, took my soup away, and replaced it with a new bowlful. Damn flies! They are everywhere.

Ralph and I have started to think about what it will be like to be home. How are we going to adjust to not being able to having a beer (or two), and a half-bottle of good wine, each day—to say nothing of dessert?

Though our mileage was longer today, it was not a tiring one—fewer hills to climb. I was pleased to end the day feeling comfortable, rather than in my usual clammy, sweaty state. We're staying at the Hotel O'Pino. Our room is generously sized and decorated luxuriously. The headboard is covered with padded damask with a rose design. Because we are upstairs, we can look out above the street to groves of eucalyptus. It seems so strange to encounter another similarity to the landscape of California, Australia's famous trees, on this continent. Here, however, the trees are put to use for furniture and paper, whereas at home they are generally considered worthless, even dangerous, because they burn and explode rapidly during wildfires.

After we settled in at the hotel, we walked the mile into Arca. We stopped at the local refugio to get another *cello* (rubber stamp) on our credentials. We have one more to go to have the page filled. (It holds up to 40 stamps, but one that we earlier collected takes up 2 spaces.)

WE HAVE TEN to twelve miles to go tomorrow, depending on our route. Incredible! We will have walked more than 400 miles. What will we do for an encore? It's almost a scary thought.

We both expected to lose all kinds of weight (not that Ralph needed to), but I don't think we have. We've eaten too well. I am in better shape physically, however. My legs and rear are more firm. The pain in my calves has decreased markedly. At the beginning of the trip, the pain in my legs (particularly my right one) kept me awake many nights. I had to ice them and use ibuprofen. Now, I notice pain only occasionally; I wish I knew what is going on.

There are a couple of things I won't miss at trip's end. One is having our wet laundry hanging all over the room each night. And the second is the amount of cleavage shown on TV. Even though I watch a fair amount of TV at home and have certainly seen plunging necklines before, the "sex sells" seems even more pervasive here than at home. Revealing dress is worn not just by celebrities and TV personalities, it extends to TV anchors, weather reporters, and the like. Perhaps I'm just noticing it more now because of the contrast between how the women on TV dress and how the women who labor on their farms in the villages do.

Santiago Cathedral.

14 • Santiago de Compostela

Journey's End

The desire accomplished is sweet to the soul.
—Bible (Proverbs 37:19)

JOURNAL, DAY 34 (Thursday, October 4): **A Rúa (next door to Arca) to Santiago de Compostela (12.5 miles/20 km).**

THIS WAS TO be both the last day of hiking and the climax of the trip: arriving in Santiago, reaching the old Cathedral, and receiving our certificates of completion. We set out this morning in eager anticipation. We passed through the town of Lavacolla, a town of great importance to early pilgrims because it was where they would stop and bathe before entering Santiago.

To those of us accustomed to daily showers, it is amazing to consider that early Christians rarely bathed and travelers not at all. Therefore, the rituals of bathing and purification at Lavacolla were significant. Now Lavacolla serves pilgrims primarily as Santiago's airport, and travelers on foot have to make their way around it.

We came to *Monte del Gozo* (Mount of Joy), so named because it was the first place from which pilgrims could see the towers of the cathedral of Santiago. One can only begin to imagine the joy with which the early pilgrims would have regarded it. As difficult as this journey has been for me, and to a lesser degree for Ralph, it's nothing compared to the struggles and dangers the medieval travelers would have faced. Pilgrims would race from Lavacolla to be the first to reach the top of Monte del Gozo, the last hill to climb on the way to Santiago. The winner would be entitled to the title "King." Of the scene at the summit, we have many accounts. The rapture of the pilgrims was expressed with such phrases as "they fell to their knees with tears of joy" and "they commenced to sing hymns of praise."

SADLY, THE MOUNT of Joy is far different today from what it was centuries ago. In anticipation of pilgrims flocking to Compostela in the Holy Year 1993, a large complex was constructed with accommodations for almost 3,000 people. In addition to the dozens of single-story dormitories (most with bunks for eight), there's an amphitheater, restaurants, parking lots, laundry, and so forth. Buses run on schedule to Santiago.

Though most would agree that this complex serves a useful purpose, and that the facilities are clean and comfortable, we were left wondering if the buildings erected on this site of such historical significance could not have been designed with greater artistic sensibility. Then, after making our way through that austere settlement, we reached the suburbs of Santiago. There we found that towering new apartments and office buildings block the views of the old city. Our first glimpse of the cathedral would have to wait another couple of hours until we reached the center of the old town.

JOURNAL, DAY 34, resumes: The entrance into Santiago was long, through drab commercial avenues, much like the industrial newer sections of other large cities, but our excitement carried us along. There are two approaches to the center of old town: the main road (shorter) or continuing on the way-marked Camino. The Camino route passes various chapel and historical sites; we were too intent on getting to the cathedral to stop at any.

We have arrived! Today's hike was longer than we anticipated, but we're here. We stopped first in the *Plaza del Obradoira*, Compostela's main square, which is in front of the cathedral on the west side. The cathedral is indeed impressive and grand. It more than filled the camera's viewfinder. We had to back up into the square to be able to see it all at one time and to take our initial photos.

From the plaza, we walked up the cathedral's wide steps. The first thing one notices is that the staircase is unique: the double staircase leads visitors up the steps on a zigzag route. It was built in the 17th century and designed by Fernando de Casa y Novoa. His goal was to enhance a new façade for the cathedral in the Baroque style. We entered the cathedral through the main entrance, the *Puerta de la Gloria*.

We followed others—millions if you count all of its history—to perform the traditional pilgrim acts. Just inside the entrance, we stopped to place our hands on a marble column known as the *Tree of Jesse*, which supports the statue of St. James. We contemplated how many pilgrims it has taken to wear inch-deep fingerprints into the column.

Next we watched as others proceeded to the center of the cathedral, stopped before the altar, and then climbed the few steps behind it to touch the Baroque statue of Santiago. We followed suit. Finally, we went downstairs to view the silver casket that is believed to hold his remains.

THE CHURCHES THAT preceded the present-day cathedral were much more modest. As stated earlier, the present-day site is that of chapel built in the ninth century to contain the remains of St. James. About 899, Alfonso III of León replaced that small chapel with a larger one in response to the increasing number of pilgrims coming to the site. In 997, a Muslim army under the leadership of Almanzor invaded Compostela and destroyed much of the city, including the church. In 1003, a new church was built to replace the previous one. Then, in the late 11th century, that church was torn down, and the cathedral was begun. It was consecrated in 1105.

Through the intervening centuries, several modifications have been made: chapels added, the cloister rebuilt in the 16th century, the bell tower and the remarkable double staircase in the 17th century, and the Obradoiso façade added in the 18th century.

The Cathedral

As you have traveled the Camino, you have been introduced to many of the important saints and others whose statues or paintings you will see in the cathedral. One of these is a statue of Santo Domingo (to whom you were introduced in the town of Santo Domingo de la Calzada). It is in the third chapel to the right of the Holy Door (from the inside). Though he was never a priest, he is honored in the cathedral because of his service to pilgrims. He is represented here as a strong and determined man holding a bridge with his right hand and with a chicken at his feet.

JOURNAL RESUMES: WE went to the Pilgrim Office, in the *Casa Del Dean*, to obtain our *Compostelas*. The certificates are written in Latin and acknowledge completion of the pilgrimage. Our worry about being quizzed about our motives for making the pilgrimage was unnecessary, as it turned out. We were given a register to sign and simply had to check under "for religious reasons" or "for other reasons." Undoubtedly, there are too many pilgrims for the office to deal with on an individual basis. We were told that pilgrims who arrived today will be recognized at the 12:00 mass in the cathedral tomorrow. That means we'll have a chance for some reunions. The *botafumeiro*, the giant incense burner, will be swung on Saturday.

We became tourists again. We went to look in souvenir shops and to wander through vendors' stands. We've not wanted to buy any gifts for people at home until now because we would've had to carry whatever we purchased.

For dinner, we chose a restaurant that served paella; I can't get enough of it. After recognizing a few fellow Camino travelers, we decided we'd return to the cathedral tomorrow for the special mass

We had to figure out how to return to Madrid on Saturday evening. We located the local Iberia sales office. We showed the travel agent our *Compostelas* and were happy to receive quite a discount on our flight because we came as pilgrims. It was about a 50% reduction over the regular fare.

Holy Year

The celebration of Holy Year begins months before January 1st of the given year. In fact, the festivities begin on September 22, at noon, 100 days before. Notable guests—religious and others—from Spain, France, Germany, Italy, and other countries, attend a banquet at the Reyes Católicos Parador in Obradeiro. The banquet is followed by musical and other entertainment in the squares surrounding the Cathedral.

Whereas in other years visitors enter the cathedral from the *Plaza del Obradoira* through the *Pórtico de la Gloria* on the west side, during Holy Years, they are allowed to enter through the Holy Door, also known as the *Puerta del Perdón*, on the east side. In Holy Years, it is opened by the Archbishop at 12:01 on January 1 and closed at midnight on December 31.

JOURNAL, DAY 35 (Friday, October 5): **Santiago de Compostela.**

WELL, I GUESS my expectations were too high because I am feeling let down. It rained today, so our explorations were limited. Mass was at noon. We wanted to sit, so we went early. The service was in Spanish, but we could understand that they were having communion. I think they gave the count of the number of pilgrims by their nationality, but I didn't hear "Estados Unidos." I was disappointed that our names were not called. We recognized about ten people, including the German and Australian couples.

We're staying at the Hotel Suzo. Our meals have been good; the churros served with hot chocolate here at the bar are incredible. We've also tried and enjoyed the Galician soup and *Salmón a la plancha* (Salmon to the Plate; pan-seared).

We visited the *Museo de las Peregrinaciones* (Museum of the Pilgrims). The exhibits portray the history of the cathedral as it has evolved through the ages. We learned that 20,000 people made a pilgrimage in August of 2001, but we don't know from what starting point.

We returned to the shops near the cathedral. We spent a long time looking before I found a tee-shirt that I liked showing the route of the Camino. On the plaza on the south side of the cathedral, the *Plaza de Las Platerías*, where *plata* (silver) goods have been offered by craftsmen for hundreds of years, we found replicas of the *botafumeiro* in every souvenir shop. We selected an ornament-sized one for this year's Christmas tree. We also spent a lot of time standing in the rain while Ralph studied our wet maps. I'm feeling edgy because we're not getting any exercise. Does it sound as if I'm ready to go home?

JOURNAL, DAY 36 (Saturday, October 6): **Last Visit to the Cathedral of Santiago de Compostela.**

RALPH AND I returned to the cathedral to participate in the noontime pilgrim mass. We'd been told in the pilgrims' office that we would be able to observe the ceremonial swinging of the *botafumeiro*. (The giant incense burner is also called a censer.) We'd read that in the Middle Ages the *botafumeiro* was used to fumigate the assembled pilgrims (or to cover the smell of sweat because they did not often bathe).

Although the cathedral was much more crowded than it had been when we'd arrived on Thursday, Ralph and I managed to find seats on a pew on one of the arms of the transept. Not being Catholic, Ralph and I had no idea what to expect during the ceremony.

The sanctuary of the cathedral is shaped like a cross. The long section, which leads to the altar, is the nave. The shorter section is the transept. Where the nave and the transept intersect is the main altar, the heart of the cathedral, under which the *Tomb of St. James the Apostle* lies.

THE HIGHLIGHT CAME near the end of the service. Three priests solemnly approached the main altar and then carefully tied the immense silver incense burner with a very thick rope. Eight men gathered to lift it; then they pulled it up towards the ceiling and set it swinging back and forth. As luck would have it, we were directly beneath the botafumeiro as it traveled in an arc above the altar. It was stunning.

It was not just the sight of the massive vessel swinging back and forth, the pendulum dropping lower and lower with each pass. It was even more than the swirling vapors trailing from the huge censer. It was the *sound*, the roaring swo-o-sh, sw-o-o-sh as the powerful incense burner made its long traverse above our heads. Tears came to my eyes. Others dabbed at their faces, or made the sign of the cross.

...THE BEAUTIFUL, MAGNIFICENT journey was over.

Madrid's Plaza Mayor.

The ambassador's carriage.

15 • Madrid

Trip's End

Bang, whang, whang goes the drum, tootle-te-tootle the fife.
Oh, a day in the city-square, there is no such pleasure in life!
—Robert Browning (*Up at a Villa—Down in a City*)

JOURNAL, DAY 36, resumes: **Afternoon Flight to Madrid.**

FROM SANTIAGO DE Compostela we took the hour-long flight on Iberia Airlines to bring us back to Madrid to stay again at Hotel Paris. The significant reduction on our airfare had allowed us to enjoy a much less tiring trip than a return trip by train or bus would've been. Once again I was able to enjoy the large bath-tubs of the older European hotel by soaking in the steaming hot water. Of course we washed our laundry at the same time and then hung it all over the room to add to the ambiance!

JOURNAL, DAY 37 (Sunday, October 7): **Back in Madrid**

THIS MORNING WE went a few blocks out of the city center to *El Rastro,* which has been described as one of the best flea markets in the world. It's a regular Sunday event, and has been in existence since the Middle Ages. Its hub is the *Plaza de Cascorro*; the main street is called *Calle Ribera de Curtidores* (Tanner's Riverbank) because the area originally was the slaughterhouse and tanning district.

185

The marketplace fills the streets of several city blocks. Vendors offer a tremendous range of goods, new and old, from art to lampshades, padlocks to CDs. Similar categories of merchandise are located in distinct areas. Clothing is a major section. There, hawkers call out to attract customers to their stands to buy such items as blue jeans and sweat pants. Equally crowded were the aisles displaying bras and panties. Another area was allocated to jewelry stands where costume as well as estate jewelry was displayed. Leather goods, from tiny coin purses to jackets, were offered.

Down a side street were vast collections of paintings and prints in their gilt-covered frames. Nearby was a row of tables covered with paisley-print bedspreads and heaped with CDs, tapes, packets of incense, and posters. Other side streets had become the temporary home of suppliers of plumbing supplies, outdoor gear, and electrical equipment. Roving vendors offered multi-packs of batteries. All seemed to be under the watchful eye of the local police; we noticed licenses being carefully checked.

JOURNAL, DAY 37, resumes: Coming back through the Plaza Mayor, we strolled past the stamp and coin dealer tables. There was plenty of activity around the many tables set up for the regular Sunday event. I remembered that my backpacking friend Marcy had sent an e-mail message asking, "If you see any stamps on envelopes...lying in the trash can... unwanted, unloved, tear them off and save them for me!" but I didn't know what to choose.

Madrid has several beautiful parks; we walked a distance to one called Casa de Campo. What a place! First of all, it's huge. There were thousands of people enjoying the park: listening to music, viewing art, watching performance art, having lunch over beer, bicycling, roller blading.

Music was seemingly everywhere. An orchestra was giving a Sunday concert at the bandstand; groups of traveling musicians were scattered at several locations. We heard small groups playing Andean music and rock-and-roll, individuals playing guitar.

A sculpture exhibit along the main promenade was drawing a lot of interest. We made our way over to see it, then strolled along another wide pathway, which was lined with tarot readers, mimes, and puppeteers. My favorite performance was by a couple sprayed with and dressed in white from head to toe. They were dancing the tango. They would begin their brief performance when a coin was dropped in a hat, and then freeze mid-step awaiting the next contribution.

Ralph was intrigued by a fountain with the statue of Lucifer, which according to the sign, is the world's only statue of the devil.

Madrid

Capital city, home to more than three million people, Madrid sits approximately in the geographical center of Spain and is on the arid, high-plateau known as the *meseta*. It became Spain's capital in 1561 under the rule of Felipe II. The heart of the city, Old Madrid, which stretches from the Plaza de la Villa to Puerta del Sol (Gateway of the Sun), is a vibrant center. The Plaza de la Villa is adjacent to the Town Hall and has several historic buildings including the Torre De Los Lujanes that dates from the 1400s.

The Puerta del Sol, which is about eight blocks east along Calle Mayor, is a lively square filled with shops and cafes. It's the center of Spain's cafe society, the place to see and to be seen. You'll know you are there when you see the *Tio Pepe* (a brand of sherry) sign, which overlooks the plaza. On December 31, huge crowds gather to celebrate the New Year, just as Americans do in Times Square. Tradition calls for the revelers to eat a grape with each stroke of the clock in the 1866 clock tower of the Ministry of the Interior.

Within this central district is the Plaza Mayor, which was constructed in the 1600s during the rule of the Hapsburgs. Three-story buildings surround the square, which has been the scene of bullfights, royal celebrations, inquisitions, and executions.

JOURNAL, DAY 37, resumes: I'm so happy that we returned to Madrid. It enabled me to reevaluate my initial impressions of the city. The days at the beginning of the trip weren't nearly as much fun; now I know that I can attribute that primarily to the effects of jet lag.

At lunch we had a delicious salad—a half-pineapple scooped out and filled with chunks of pineapple, shrimp, hard-boiled egg, and red peppers—all blended with a sweetened Thousand Island dressing. That delicious dish was followed by paella (it wasn't particularly exciting), chocolate cake, and bread. And, of course, beer. All this for around seven dollars; I couldn't believe the low prices.

The Spanish Inquisition

During the three and a half centuries it lasted (until 1834, when it was abolished), the Spanish Inquisition was responsible for the torture and/or death of millions of people. It began during the rule of King Fernando and Queen Isabel in 1480. Officially, the goal was to create a strong country unified by Catholicism. Protestant "heretics," as well as those who were believed to be pretending to be converts from Judaism or Islam, were brought to trial. Those accused were dragged before the court without counsel or any notice of the charges brought against them. Often they were imprisoned and tortured in order to obtain confessions and repentance, or beheaded, hanged, or burned at the stake.

Beyond the widely-stated reasons for the Inquisition, there were powerful financial considerations. First of all, those accused (or their relatives) were required to pay the expenses of their imprisonment, tortures, and trials. If the prisoners were convicted of heresy, the Spanish government acquired their financial holdings. More than one researcher has concluded that this practice provided good motivation to find the accused guilty.

While nowadays visitors will find the Plaza Mayor a bit more peaceful, it's still the scene of many a pageant, parade, or state ceremony. The street-level, arched porticoes are filled with shops and outdoor cafes. Art students and other artists can be seen seated before their easels practicing their craft. A collectors' market is held in the plaza on Sundays; stamps, coins, sometimes books and magazines may be found.

JOURNAL RESUMES: TONIGHT we went to *Inglés*, one of Madrid's major department stores. While Ralph searched for something in English to read while on the airplane, I bought the last gifts we needed: a small picture frame for my soon-to-be daughter-in-law, Anne, a tiny bedside clock for my friend Jean, and colorful, lacy fans for several other friends. The venture took us out when thousands of others were similarly shopping, eating, and visiting; the shopping boulevards were filled wall to wall with people.

We found an Internet cafe so we could read the news and check our e-mails. We learned that the U.S. and Britain have bombed strategic sites in Afghanistan. The only good news seems to be the continued support and solidarity of so many other countries. Leaders in France, Canada, Australia, and Germany seem to feel the bombings are justified and needed. They are in agreement that this terrorism needs to be stopped. One wonders how it can ever be brought to an end. We are also dropping humanitarian supplies of food and medicine for the people of Afghanistan. "Will they get it?" is always the question. We can only hope. Boy, will I be glad to get home!

WHILE IN MADRID, we were lucky weather-wise. We enjoyed clear, sunny skies with temperatures in the 70s daytime, 60s at nighttime. But since Madrid is in the meseta and has a continental climate, the weather can be brutal. Temperatures may reach the freezing point during the months of December through February, and hit more than 85 F. (30 C.) in July and August. When much of Europe suffered from a heat wave in summer 2003, Madrid sweltered with weeks of temperatures exceeding 100 degrees Fahrenheit.

JOURNAL, DAY 38 (Monday, Oct. 8): **Our last day in Madrid.**

CHOCOLATE SO THICK you can literally eat it with a spoon—like homemade chocolate pudding before it cools—that's what you get when you order chocolate with churros here. Why has this treat not made its way to the New World?

We made our way back to the official residence of the King. We'd hoped to go on a tour, but the gates were closed to visitors. We noticed crowds gathering nearby and went to investigate. There on the concrete roadways below us we could see soldiers in parade dress marching smartly in formation. Black carriages—one embellished with the royal coat of arms—decorated with bright-red spoked wheels and trimmed with gold—were pulled into the official procession by a pair of brown horses wearing feathered plumes on their heads. Stately cars pulled into the line.

We craned our necks to see what the "to-do" was all about. No one in the scene below seemed concerned by the increasing numbers of on-lookers on the overpass for a while, but when the entourage of people in their finery began to be escorted to a waiting carriage, sirens of approaching police cars cut through the peaceful setting. Uniformed policemen hurried to cordon off the overlook where we had been enjoying the romantic scene.

Still, we could see the ranks of soldiers on horseback, the marching rows of the bands and their crisp uniforms of purple, green, black, red and white.

We still had no idea why the pomp and circumstance. We watched until our interest waned, then made our way back to the Plaza Mayor for one last look before returning to our nearby hotel. We had hardly arrived when the plaza began to buzz with excitement. Into view came the procession once again; we heard that one of the carriages was carrying a new ambassador to introduce to King Juan Carlos I.

...WE FLEW HOME on Tuesday, October 9, 2001.

16 • Reflections

Twenty years from now you will be more disappointed by the things you didn't do than by the ones you did do. So throw off the bowlines. Sail away from the safe harbor. Catch the trade winds in your sail. Explore. Dream. Discover.

—Mark Twain

Throughout the few years intervening between our journey on the Camino and the publication of this book, I have participated in many author's events: talks, readings, slide shows, and book fairs promoting my book on women's backpacking. Also, while I was busy writing this book on the Camino de Santiago, Ralph and I gave several presentations on our pilgrimage. In the question-and-answer period that usually follows these programs, several questions were frequently asked that I would like to address here:

How did walking the Camino affect your life?

AFTER OUR TRIP, I gave some thought to how the Camino hike had changed me. I was aware that many, if not most, people who have traveled the Camino have reported feeling profoundly affected by their experience. Many people taking this historic pilgrimage are in a time of transition: they've just graduated from college and haven't found their first job, an important relationship has come unraveled and they want time to process their experience, or they've just retired and are wondering what to do in their next stage of life. Others are searching for answers to age-old questions: "What is the meaning of life?" "What is my purpose here on Earth?" And, because walking the Camino is intertwined with religious tradition, many are drawn to it to broaden their spiritual understandings.

I didn't feel that I was searching for resolution of any of these questions. Though I *had* just retired, I was very happy with my life. I was primarily hoping for an interesting vacation that would provide better physical fitness as an added benefit. Still, I wondered if I would have some sort of transformational experience.

It HAS BEEN said that the Camino lies directly under the Milky Way and follows ley lines that reflect the energy from those star systems above it. On her website (www.shirley-maclaine.com), Shirley MacLaine asserts that the Camino is a sacred site with the power to transform. She compares ley lines running through the earth to chi running through the human body and believes that both are spiritual life forces. Others have stated that *El Santiago de Compostela* (or St. James' Way) is like the "Milky Way," that there were as many pilgrims on the path as there are stars in the sky.

Yet in the first weeks after our trip, I felt there'd been little impact beyond what our earlier vacations to Peru, Bolivia, Mexico, Hawaii, and other interesting places have provided. After all, those exotic locales also have beautiful scenery, vibrant cultures, and fascinating histories. But, though our other vacations have involved a fair amount of physical activity (hiking, snorkeling), the Camino had been a much more demanding trip: physically, mentally, and emotionally. Later, I had second thoughts.

How did you survive six weeks of togetherness?

As I reflected on our trip, I realized that the way that Ralph and I dealt with the challenges of the Camino may be of benefit to others setting out. Travel writer extraordinaire Paul Theroux has stated that he will not even read a travel writer whose work begins with such words as: "My husband/wife/companion/friend and I...." He maintains that only *solo* travel provides the adventures and insights he is searching for. He is adamantly opposed to someone else pointing things out to him.

IN SPAIN, OUR style of travel was contrary to Theroux's preferences: Ralph and I frequently pointed out things of interest to each other. Our conversations reflected our surroundings—whether it was the changing vegetation as we moved from mountain to valley to plain or the rich carvings and paintings in a church. We enjoyed stopping to share a sighting of a monstrous spider web, an egret rising from a canal, or a colorful sunrise.

I have traveled both with and without Ralph, sometimes on my own, sometimes with other people. I know that traveling with a companion makes for a different experience than traveling alone does. When you travel with someone, you tend to focus on that person (or group). Your perceptions are shared with them—perhaps filtered through theirs.

Many people prefer that which is familiar and safe, but others find such travel confining, even boring. Some people believe that traveling with others so isolates you from your surroundings that one place is much like another....

When you travel alone, you are much more likely to interact with the locals—you're forced to. You don't have a ready-made companion. You have to make your own fumbling attempts to communicate—sometimes in languages not well known.

There are other advantages, and disadvantages, to

traveling solo. An advantage is that your time is your own: the times to eat, stroll, and sleep are entirely at your pleasure (keeping in mind the schedules of such things as restaurants and trains). But the downside may be that you miss out on being with, and intimately sharing experiences with, someone whose company you presumably enjoy.

Ralph and I usually travel together as a matter of preference. I'm lucky. My husband is easy to travel with, and I'm fairly easy. Truth be told, he rarely complains, and I'm free to. Ralph and I have traveled together many times in the nineteen years we have been together. Most of our trips have been closer to adventure trips rather than luxury tours. (We first met at the beginning of a car-caravan camping trip to Baja California; my first backpacking trip, to climb Mt. Whitney, was three months after we were married; our week-long vacations usually take us to California's high Sierra.) When we embarked on the pilgrimage in Spain, however, it was a first in many respects.

One of the major differences we faced was that it would involve being together constantly—often in circumstances that were stressful—for six weeks. With my greater need for "down time" or "leave me alone!" time, I wondered how this amount of time together would play out.

During the trip, I occasionally reflected on how it was that Ralph and I managed the extended time together. I realized that our individual ways of creating needed personal space had evolved. We have learned how to be together constantly, yet have time alone.

This isn't as contradictory as it sounds: it begins with respect for each other's needs. Though sometimes we walked and talked together, much of the time we walked separately with one or the other of us about ten feet ahead, which gave us both a break. I'm the one who needs more time for contemplation, and if I really wanted to be able to reflect on my surroundings, or thoughts, I'd ask Ralph to stay an even greater distance behind me. I found that when he walked just behind me, his footsteps could be distracting; I felt the tension of having someone passing. Sometimes I walked a bit behind him; it allowed me to walk along in more of a daze, knowing that someone ahead was sort of shielding me.

RALPH SATISFIED HIS need for personal space in a non-physical way. He isn't distracted by my being right on his heels, or right ahead of him, but he appreciated the fact that I didn't demand constant conversation. He's a quiet person. He enjoys my company, and he likes hearing my comments, but he doesn't want to be required to converse non-stop.

It's important to be able to walk at your own pace. It's uncomfortable to be pressured to walk faster and it's no fun to be held back. Because my pace is slower than Ralph's, except on uphill stretches, we have had to reach some kind of accommodation or I would be walking alone the greater part of the day (some couples are okay with that; we are not).

Over time we found a solution that worked for us; it became automatic. Ralph walked at his own rate but stopped frequently (giving himself a break) to wait for me. If *I* had to make a stop to adjust my backpack or tie a shoelace, he waited for me. When *he* needed to stop to shed a jacket, etc., I continued on ahead, knowing that he'd catch up with me fairly soon and that I'd saved him from one of those "Wait for me!" calls.

WE FOUND OTHER ways to take time for ourselves, even when together 24/7. We read. We wrote in our journals. We took photographs. All were quiet opportunities for putting aside other thoughts or chores and getting to relax.

Finally, Ralph and I often met people on the trail. We shared meals and lodgings with the other pilgrims. In that manner, we were able to enjoy the company of others and be ourselves. There will always be both advantages and disadvantages to traveling with a companion, or not. There are many paths to Santiago....

How do I find someone with whom to hike?

First of all, consider that it is *not* necessary to find a hiking partner. In fact, if you don't have one already, I'd recommend you consider starting your hike alone. Many people we met while on the Camino (and on various long-distance trails over the years) started out by themselves and soon found others to hike with. Many people hike with others for a while and then strike out on their own. Make it *your* hike!

But if you want to find a hiking partner, the methods are similar to those used for finding a date. Ask friends, co-workers, and relatives for ideas; go places where others hang out (such as on local hikes); check out Internet backpacking forums (i.e. *Backpacker Magazine's* community forums at www.backpacker.com, and other chatlines); place an ad in appropriate newspapers (e.g., Sierra Club bulletin); put a notice on a bulletin board (at your local outdoor supply or sporting goods store); or signup for a trip (Sierra Club, Women's Adventures, etc.).

Also, you can subscribe to my free, e-mailed newsletter by e-mailing us at backpack45@yahoo.com. In my twice-monthly newsletter, I occasionally forward information about hiking groups and adventure companies who sound reliable and whose trips sound interesting.)

If you determine that you want a hiking partner from the outset and have a candidate, you'll want to make sure they'll be *compatible* for long-distance hiking. This may be challenging, but since you are establishing a relationship—and hiking one, two, or six weeks with someone constitutes a relationship—you want it to be a good one.

Discuss each person's expectations of the trip. Do you want to spend several layover days in some of the major cities? Does your companion want to visit every church along the way? Do you both want to stay in refugios, or in small hotels? Will you be usually be cooking in the refugios or eating out? Go on a dayhike together. Do you walk at similar rates? Can you agree on how long a hiking day should be?

It's much wiser to consider these issues ahead of time. Iron out the differences at home and you won't have so many surprises on the trail. When considering compatibility issues, perhaps Ralph's and my experiences that I've mentioned earlier will be illustrative.

How did 9/11 affect your Camino hike?

Like most Americans, we were filled with sorrow over the deaths, injuries, and destruction caused by the explosions of 9/11. We were anxious to find out why they had occurred, who was to blame, and frightened about what might happen next. Having limited access to the news was stressful to us, but clearly those at home found it stressful to have constant replays of the collapsing Twin Towers and so forth.

I was torn between wanting to fly home and be with loved ones and wanting to carry on with some normality. The fact that airports were far distant, were closed for a few days in the aftermath of the attacks, and were less safe than where we were, made the decision to continue as planned relatively easy. In the process, we probably responded as most Americans did; we tried to sort out what was happening in our country as we considered how best to continue with our own lives.

It was strange to be as insignificant as any one stone placed along the route, and to seem so far removed from events in the U.S., yet be able to quickly contact family and friends at home by using the Internet cafes. I was extremely thankful that we had that means of communication.

Is hiking the Camino safe?

In the question-and-answer period that follows our Camino program, the concern about safety, spoken or unspoken, often arose. In my opinion, the question is really whether it is safer to be in Spain, or on the Camino, or at home. And answering that question would require a crystal ball. Terrorists and the perceived threat of terrorists seem to be today's reality. In historical perspectives, it's likely safer to be on the Camino today than it has been over many of the centuries of the trail's existence.

Obviously being on the Camino during September 2001 made our walk more of an adventure than we had anticipated. Not only were the events of 9/11 totally unexpected, they also shattered our collective illusions that America is safe from terrorist acts.

But after the initial days where everyone—friends and family back home and we abroad—watched to see just what had happened and waited to see what would happen next, Ralph and I figured that being in rural Spain was about the safest place in the world to be. While those stateside were glued to their TV sets or followed other news outlets for days, Ralph and I were walking across the meseta where there was limited access to news coverage.

THERE ARE THOSE who use the relative newsworthiness and high profile of the Camino and the city of Santiago for their own means. In 2003, there were train bombings in Madrid and subsequent small explosions in Compostela and other cities. There was some speculation that Basque Separatist groups were responsible, but they, unlike with previous attacks, denied responsibility. (In fact, in March, 2006, the Basque separatist group ETA declared a "permanent" cease fire and promised to end years of violence.)

IN NOVEMBER 2004, various news media reported that the

attacks on Madrid and elsewhere had been linked to the terrorist group, Al Queda. However, in March, 2006, it was determined that those responsible were Islamic radicals, but that there was no Al Queda connection.

FOUR YEARS LATER: *How has hiking the Camino affected your life?*

Four years after our hike, one of our closest friends, Bob Doerr, asked me for a second time, "How did hiking the Camino affect you, or change your life?" Although initially I didn't think it had affected me much at all (beyond, as previously mentioned) any other trip to an exciting destination, I now realize that over time, it has affected Ralph and me greatly.

For me, this trip brought forth many thoughts and emotions similar to other significant journeys in my life such as writing and self-publishing my first book in 1980, getting divorced and being on my own for the first time in my mid-40s, and going backpacking for the first time when I was 48. And, as with these past journeys, my life was to be transformed once again.

FIRST OF ALL, when we realized that we could walk long-distance trails, it opened up a whole new world of possibilities. Rather than two people who have gone on a single long hike, we have become long-distance hikers. After we hiked on the Camino de Santiago, we began taking increasingly longer hikes in the Sierra. We decided we would attempt to complete the entire Pacific Crest Trail (a 2,650-mile trail that goes from the Mexican border to the Canadian border through the highest mountain ranges of California, Oregon, and Washington).

Then, in 2004 and 2005, we went to France and hiked on the *Vía Podensis* (aka GR 65), a 500-mile trail that begins in Le Puy-en-Velay (one of the four French trails that leads into the Way of St. James). Our goal is to continue on into the Pyrenees through St. Jean-Pied-de-Port to Roncesvalles (our original starting point). Then we plan to travel (by public transportation) to León in order to hike the 100-mile stretch between there and Ponferrada that we had to skip over in 2001.

SECOND, OUR EXPERIENCES on the Camino led me to write this book. My usual method of preparing for a trip isn't for everyone; I tend to choose the destination, consider how I can learn the language on the flight over, and exchange a few bills for the local currency. I'm very good at setting up our travel arrangements, good enough at getting our household affairs in order, and excellent at packing light. I am terrible at actually researching the political and cultural background and history of the place I'm going.

Upon arrival at our destination, I finally stop and look around. If Ralph and I are staying in a hotel, we usually try to get our bearings by walking in one direction and reading all the signs and exploring all the shops along the way. The next time out, we head out in a different direction. We continue our explorations until we run out of time. In large cities one sometimes has to use public transit or a taxi cab, but I find that to be a more difficult way to gain a sense of direction. On foot, I am more quickly able to immerse myself in the place where I am staying.

Often my method of living in the moment works well for me. But sometimes, as on the trip to Spain, it dawns on me that perhaps a bit more time spent researching our destination ahead of time would have been in order. If I wanted to better understand Spain's past and present, I needed to learn more about it than I could pick up by wandering through city streets and museums.

IN RETROSPECT, I see that my life has been enriched and changed in all-encompassing ways by our Camino pil-

grimage. The changes—physically, mentally, and spiritually—were subtle in the short term, profound in the long.
Physically, I learned that I was stronger than I thought I was.
I gained confidence in my ability to do further explorations,
which subsequently led to the long-distance hikes both here
and abroad. *Mentally*, I learned during the pilgrimage and
from my research afterwards a great deal more about the
history and culture of Spain than I had known before. And
spiritually, I sensed a connection, a tie, to the millions who
had traveled our path before or will travel it in the years
ahead. It was a comfort to know others had walked the
walk; it is gratifying to know that my journey has encouraged and inspired others.

This book is largely the result of what I have studied. I
realized, partly because of my own experience, that I
needed to delve deeper into the traditions and history of
Spain and its Camino. From the rich and complex history
of Spain, I've enjoyed gathering many of the legends and
much of the background information needed to fully understand why millions have been drawn to the Camino
de Santiago and Santiago de Compostela (which became a
UNESCO World Heritage Site in 1985).

WHATEVER FORM YOUR Camino pilgrimage takes, I wish you
a safe and rewarding journey.
    Buen Camino!
    Susan

A *Rollo* (judicial post) for hanging criminals.

17 • How to Prepare for Your Camino Trip

Tying up the Loose Ends

Worry is like a rocking chair; it gives you something to do, but it doesn't get you anywhere.

—Anonymous (www.aphids.com)

Once you decide where you want to begin and where you want to end your pilgrimage, your journey becomes clear and exciting.

Gateways to the Camino: *Traveling from Madrid, Paris, or London*

THOSE PLANNING TO hike the entire Spanish portion of the Camino have several options of how to get to the commonly-used starting points of Roncesvalles, Spain or St. Jean-Pied-de-Port, France—both in the Pyrenees. As you'll discover, there are a few alternatives—each with its advantages and disadvantages.

Those traveling from **Madrid** usually take the train to Pamplona. (The Spanish National Railways, RENFE, posts current schedules and fares at www.renfe.es.) From Pamplona you'll find a local bus that leaves daily (schedule varies on Sunday) to Roncesvalles. (This is the route that Ralph and I took.) If you want your trip to start on the French side of the border, in St. Jean-Pied-de-Port, you can take a cab from Pamplona or Roncesvalles.

THOSE COMING FROM **Paris** will take the TGV (*train a grande vitesse*/high-speed train) to Bayonne (reservations required, but can be made in advance by Internet, etc.), then transfer in Bayonne to the local train to St. Jean-Pied-de-Port. As of this writing, there are two daytime departures and one overnight from Paris to Bayonne; there are five trains from Bayonne to St. Jean-Pied-de-Port. You're able to make reservations for *both* parts of the *overnight* trip (departing Paris about 11:00 PM), so even though you will have to transfer to another train, you will already have your ticket for the second train. For details and other options, go to http://www.sncf.com/indexe.htm (English version).

TRAVELERS FROM **LONDON** have several choices. They can fly to the French town of Biarritz, then take the bus *(Eurolines)* to Bayonne and by train continue to St. Jean-Pied-de-Port (a one-hour ride). Alternately, they can take the bus from London directly to Bayonne (20 hours) and continue on by train. Other options include taking a short flight or ferry to Bilbao and then buses, or bus and train, to Roncesvalles or St. Jean-Pied-de-Port. Check Ryanair at www.ryanair.com for flights to Biarritz; find Easy Jet to Bilbao and Madrid at www.easyjet.com.

AT THE END of their trip to Santiago, pilgrims can return home in a number of ways. On foot, if they want to follow the custom of medieval travelers, or by air, bus, or train if they prefer to return home in a quicker, more relaxing manner. The long-distance bus/coach line, ALSA, is at www.alsa.es.

For more information comparing modes of transportation, routes, costs, seasons of service, and time schedules for travel to and from various towns and cities on the Camino, refer to *The Camino Francés*, one of the *Pilgrim Guides to Spain*, listed below.

Note: If *returning* home by public transportation, as most contemporary pilgrims do, make your return travel arrangements as early as practical—especially if you are going to be departing Santiago in the peak months of July or August. Because there is rapidly growing interest in making a pilgrimage on the Camino de Santiago and reaching Santiago, accommodations in Santiago can be difficult to find, and last-minute purchase of air, train, and bus tickets to home may be impossible.

A long with the resurgence in number of pilgrims traveling its route, there has also been a steadily increasing number of informative and inspiring books published about it. If you are going to hike the Camino, divide your reading into two stacks: books you will read before your trip (or after) and those you will carry with you on the trail. In your first stack of books, for reading before and after your trip, you will undoubtedly want to include books on art, history, and various journals and personal essays. Let your interests and budget be your guide.

The second stack should be of books with practical value—ones you will carry with you. For English speakers, there is one small essential guidebook, the aforementioned *Pilgrim Guides to Spain, 1. The Camino Francés* which is updated annually by the Confraternity of Saint James. It's published in England and should be ordered well in advance of your trip. William Bisset, the editor, does the updates using feedback from pilgrims who have recently been on the Camino.

A TYPICAL ENTRY (towns with more points of interest, or more accommodations will have lengthier entries): (2005 Guide, Page 49):

"4.5km [the number of kilometers from the previous

town] **to Molinaseca (744, 585m)** [population, elevation in meters].

"R [refuge] **(28)** [number of beds] in a chalet style converted church, 500m out of village on Ponferrada road. Cooker, sink, showers, hot water. Tents with mattresses for summer overflow. Internet. Priority to walkers. Cyclists may have to wait until after 2000 (8:00 PM). Open all year, 4 euros. Key from Alfredo, who lives next to Bodega La Rana (closed) near *Supermercado Elias* (ask for directions).

"H [hostal] *Hostal El Palacio* 987 453 094 near the bridge, 40 euros. *Las Casa del Reloj* 987 453 124, 40 euros. Good reports. *Posada de Muriel*, Plaza de San Cristo (west end of village) 987 453 201, 54 euros. Reported friendly with good *menu*. Several *mesones* doing good meals incl. *Meson del Puente Romano* by bridge, and *Rte. Azar* c/El Palacio, also several bars.

"An attractive larger village. You enter over the Romanesque Puente de Peregrinos; below it, the river is dammed in the summer to provide excellent swimming. Two shops, incl. a *supermercado*, which may not stick to advertised hours (but you are only 8 km from Ponferrada now). *Farmacia* on main road 500m before refuge."

ORDER THE PILGRIM guide from: *www.csj.org.uk* or William Bisset, Hield House, Holwick, Middleton-in-Teesdale, DL12 ONR.

As one who can get lost in the San Francisco Bay Area even though I have lived here most of my life, I found it amazing that the Camino was so well "way marked." We never lost our way. However, you will undoubtedly gain more from your pilgrimage on the Camino if you do some reading about it *before* your adventure. There are several wonderful books available—listed in this book's bibliography—many with beautiful photographs.

In addition, I recommend that travelers carry a supplementary guidebook or two that provide some historical background, some information on cultural attractions, and suggested places to eat and sleep.

We tore out and carried sections from both the *Lonely Planet Walking Guide* (about thirty-five pages of it) and about half of Gitlitz and Davidson's *Pilgrimage Road to Santiago.* We threw away pages as we traveled past the areas described and bought new copies of the books when we got home (another option is to photocopy the desired pages). Since our trip, two excellent "carry with you" guides have been published; you can choose between Davies and Cole's *Walking the Camino de Santiago* or John Brierley's *A Pilgrim's Guide to the Camino de Santiago.*

There are also helpful websites on the Internet. In fact, there are more resources for learning about this historic route now than at any other time in history. Our website *www.backpack45.com* is a good place to start since it gives both historical and practical information and provides up-to-date resources.

Logistics for Travelers

Though at first glance, this section—with its comprehensive lists—may seem overwhelming, in actuality you probably do most of these things intuitively. However, we have found that no matter how many times we have traveled, without a checklist it is quite easy to overlook some small matter that would've been much more easily handled at an earlier stage. Breaking the list into tasks requiring smaller chunks of time will make it much easier to fit your preparations into your normal routine in the few weeks preceding your trip.

Obviously, everyone taking a Camino trip will need not to consider all items. For example, if you have a housesitter, you will not need to set the timers and alarms nor move the indoor plants to one location. Do the chores a bit at a time, and let your trip be one with smooth sailing.

As Soon As You Decide on Your Itinerary

- *Purchase* airline, ship, or other transportation tickets (inquire if you will be able to get at least a partial refund if the tickets go on sale after they are initially ordered). Note that, unfortunately, airline fares for stays of 30 days and longer usually cost more than shorter visits and that sale prices seldom apply.
- *Arrange* travel-interruption insurance, if needed.

Up to three months in advance

- *Book* accommodations for lodging. We like to know where we will stay the first night and the last night; others may want more extensive arrangements. Request confirmation numbers, or at least note with whom and when, you made reservations. Note that on the Camino itself, you are not allowed to make reservations for *refugios*—it's first come, first served (though there is discussion that this may change!).
- *Sign up* for a conversational Spanish class, or study on your own with books, CDs, tapes, or TV programs. Spanish-language *telenovelas* (soap operas) use fairly predictable dialog.
- *Order* the *Pilgrim Guides to Spain, #1: The Camino Francés* for the current year from the Confraternity of Saint James office in London. Website: www.csj.org.uk or e-mail: office@csjorg.uk or telephone: (011-44) 020 7403 4500.
- *Order* or renew passport if required. (Some countries require that your passport be valid for six months from your date of arrival. Check this out.)
- *Check* with your health-care provider to see what medical immunizations are recommended. Since you will be hiking through a lot of farming areas on the Camino, be sure that you've had a tetanus vaccination within the last

ten years. Those over 50 years of age are the group *least* likely to have up-to-date tetanus immunizations, putting themselves at unnecessary risk.

- *Make* necessary doctor and dental appointments.
- *Plan* house-sitting or pet care.
- *Consider* yard maintenance. In our case, we elected to install a drip-irrigation system to simplify watering.
- *If* you are planning to buy a new camera, begin your research.
- *Revisit* your insurance requirements and update your will.
- *Stay* organized: create a file folder and keep all correspondence and trip notes in one place (including this checklist).
- *Check* the pack list on our website.
- *Purchase* footwear. If you are shopping for boots, try them on with the type of socks that you will wear on your trip. Your feet will swell, so buy boots at least a half-size larger. Allow plenty of time to break in your shoes.
- *Treat* shoes with at least two coats of water repellent, if appropriate.
- *Decide* on backpack.
- *Join* (at least) the Yahoo group "Santiagobis" to get familiar with many aspects of the trip and get advice. Sometimes you can read messages from people who are on the trip and learn about current weather conditions, refugio conditions, etc.

Gathering Information for Your Journey

WE'VE FOUND SEVERAL useful forums on the web where you can ask questions and get answers by **e-mail:**
- *www.caminosantiago.com*—this site, though based in Spain, has an excellent forum in *English.*
- *santiagobis yahoo group*: 1300+ members—good information—five to ten messages per day.

- *ultreya yahoo group*: forum is at www.ultreya.net—252 members.
- *saintjames yahoo group*: 240 members—similar to santiagobis and ultreya.
- *GoCamino* is provided by American Pilgrims on the Camino. This respected U.S. organization provides a website *at www.americanpilgrims.com*, and sponsors an annual meeting. To join the listserv, see *http://gocamino.oakapple.net*. This group is a replacement for the original gocamino run for years by Linda Davidson. The new group has the archives of the original. Also, you can obtain the pilgrim credential needed to stay in the refugios from this organization in advance of your trip. (It will also be available at major starting points such as Roncesvalles.)
- *www.groups.msn.com/ElCaminoSantiago*. This website by Grant Spangler has a wealth of information including maps, routes, train and bus schedules.

Travel and Medical Insurance

Your first step in considering travel or medical insurance will be determining how much risk you are facing financially and physically on your trip. Consider these factors:

- Money lost if your entry hotel or other place of lodging goes out of business.
- Cost and inconvenience if your backpack is lost, damaged, or stolen.
- Cost of transportation to medical facilities and subsequent hospital care.
- Monetary penalties for postponing or canceling your transportation costs to and from your destination.
- Costs incurred if your airline flight is delayed. You may need to pay for extra food and lodging; you might miss a connecting flight.

Even though in past years I have traveled blissfully unaware of the risks I was taking by not having insurance, I'm somewhat older and wiser now. I've found that for some trips, travel or medical insurance may be worthwhile. But, before you rush out to buy a new policy, check what coverage you already have. Airlines and other service providers are much less likely to refund your money than they once were.

Your homeowners insurance policy may cover your clothing and luggage, though probably not your camera or money. Check what coverage your VISA/MasterCard/American Express offers. Some cards offer continued coverage on past purchases. Supplement your existing coverage with trip cancellation insurance (TCI) unless you determine you want to self-insure.

Determine what medical coverage you already have while traveling. Carry your health plan card. Even if your policy is in effect outside your coverage area or outside of the country, you may be required to pay medical costs when service is provided and later submit a claim for your reimbursement.

If you do decide to order trip cancellation insurance, order your insurance promptly after ordering your plane tickets, etc., because after your initial enrollment most plans will not cover you for any pre-existing medical conditions. Websites offering *comparisons* of TCI include: Travel Insure (www.travelinsure.com), InsureMyTrip (www.insuremytrip.com) and Quote Travel Insurance (www.quotetravelinsurance.com).

One month in advance

- *Inventory* your clothing list and make necessary purchases.
- *Locate* money belt.
- *Enlist* trusted neighbor or house-sitting service to keep an eye on your place—to pick up the mail, to call the newspaper if they forget to stop the paper, to put the trash barrels back in place as needed, etc.
- *Determine* watering system for *indoor* plants. (Put them together in a protected spot outdoors? Buy self-watering

containers? Give them away? Ask a friend or neighbor to care for them at their place, or yours? Have a house sitter take care of them?)

- *Pack* your backpack and weigh it. With a quart of water, it shouldn't exceed twenty pounds.

Two weeks in advance

- *Prepay* utility and other regular bills (double up) that are not on-line payments.
- *Leave* a couple of pre-signed checks with a *trusted* person to send off to pay any bills that you may have overlooked.
- *Arrange* pet care, whether dog-walking services, pet boarding, or a visiting pet-sitter.
- *Arrange* newspaper vacation hold/stop. If you request, some newspapers will deliver your papers to public schools during your absence.
- *Contact* post office to have them hold mail, or arrange for a trusted person to pick-up it up.
- *Obtain* euros sufficient to pay for taxis and a middle of the night arrival. (As with many foreign countries, Spain offers limited access to banks on weekends, but ATM machines are widely available. Most ATM machines accept a *maximum* of four characters, and the keys only have numbers. If you normally remember your PIN number by letters, be sure you learn the corresponding numbers on the keys. Check the website to determine the availability of ATM machines in the areas you will be visiting. It will help you know how much cash you'll need.)
- *Update* mailing address (snail mail, e-mail), and phone number lists. Note: most European computer keyboards have a different layout than we are used to. Sending messages to friends will be easier if you create a "list" while you're still at home.
- *Make* two copies of your passport, itinerary (hotel numbers), traveler's checks, credit cards (front and back so

you'll have a contact number if needed). Leave one copy at home with a trusted person and carry one copy separate from your money and cards for your protection in case of loss or theft.

- *Put* jewelry and valuables in a bank safety-deposit box.
- *Refill* needed prescriptions (best to carry in original, labeled containers).
- *List* medical information—doctor's and dentist's phone numbers, prescriptions of drugs and eyeglasses, lists of allergies or medical conditions.

One week in advance

- *Purchase* film, camera batteries, or memory cards.
- *Inventory* and fill in needed over-the-counter (OTC) medications—Lomotil, ibuprofen, and so forth.
- *Purchase* sunscreen, toiletries, cosmetics, etc.
- *Consider* sleep mask and neck pillow for airline travel.
- *Obtain* earplugs for use in crowded refugios.
- *Get* needed supply of pet food if pets will be staying home (or leave money in the sugar bowl for food replenishment by your pet sitter).
- *Update* your security system. Give a trusted neighbor a copy of your itinerary and contact numbers. If you have a security service, be sure they have up-to-date emergency numbers. Tell them your departure and return dates if warranted. Some communities suggest notifying the local police of your absence.
- *Arrange* transportation to airport or other departure point.

Within last week

- *Confirm* flights.
- *Gather* documents of travel:
  passport (and the copy carried in a separate place);
  record of immunizations as required, travel tickets, hotel confirmations.

- *Check* yard and indoor watering systems.
- *Remove* any wet laundry from the washer or hamper.
- *Check* your refrigerator. Use or dump food that will be too old by the time you return. Fill several liter soda bottles with water and place in freezer to keep food frozen in case of a short-term brownout.
- *Clean* perishables (onions, potatoes, fruit) out of the pantry.
- *Disconnect* appliances such as the TV and VCR that consume electricity in the "ready-on" mode.
- *Set* indoor and outdoor lights for self-timing.
- *Wash* clothes.
- *Pack.* If you have a traveling companion, pack some of each other's clothing and essential items in case a backpack is delayed or lost—there will be something to wear until the other backpack is located.
- *Lock* windows and doors and shut skylights.
- *Set* radio, or similar, to play at determined times.
- *Set* alarms.

The Gear You'll Need

MONEY MATTERS
- *Moneybelt:* Around-the-waist style for passport, airline tickets, cash, credit cards, family phone numbers, etc.
- *Currency and plastic:* Minimal amount of U.S. currency for homeward-bound travel, sufficient euros to pay initial cab/shuttle/bus fare to hotel, etc. When on the Camino, we were able to find a town with an ATM machine about every two or three days. We used our debit card that also doubled as a VISA card. (Some people like to carry two different ATM/credit cards in case there's a problem with one of them.)

BASICS

- *Maps and guidebooks:* These are found in Ralph's backpack.
- *Backpack:* Ralph and I each used a Golite pack weighing about one pound empty. Loaded, we were each carrying about 15 pounds.
- *Bedding:* We carried *down* sleeping bags on our trip through Spain, but noticed that many locals carried a blanket instead. Since most refugios had blankets, we decided that a summer-weight bag (to 45° F.) would have been fine. (On our subsequent hiking trips in France, we left the down bags home and carried silk sleeping bag liners. We found them delightful.)
- *Hiking sticks:* While not essential, they help a lot on the downhill parts and when going through boggy areas. They also give you some upper-body workout while you walk. Be sure they fold or collapse.
- *Umbrella:* Compact, lightweight. Though our jackets are waterproof, it's much more pleasant to walk in the rain without water pouring on your head and getting in your face. Under drizzly conditions, using an umbrella may alleviate the necessity of changing into rain gear. Umbrellas also shield you from the sun and buffer the wind. Well worth the eight or nine ounces.
- *Bandanna:* This essential item can be used for many purposes beyond covering your head or tying around your neck. Alternately it can be a washcloth, a hankie, a picnic placemat, or a bandage. It can also be used to hold a splint in place or to wrap a sprained ankle. Don't leave home without it!

SUNDRIES

- *Eyeglasses:* Sunglasses and regular prescription.
- *Campsuds:* An all-purpose biodegradable, concentrated liquid that you can use for washing clothes, bathing, showering, and shampooing. We washed out clothes

every night.

- *Towel:* I brought a 12-inch *piece* of a Packtowel. Having such a small piece was awful; it left me feeling chilled in unheated shower rooms whenever I used it. (Find better ways to reduce your pack weight.)
- *Toiletries:* Toothbrush, toothpaste, floss, comb, prescription drugs, OTC meds such as Tums, Motrin, and Pepto-Bismol. Sunscreen, lip-gloss with sun protection (SPF 30), hand lotion, and disposable razor. Optional: lipstick, cosmetics.
- *Bandages and tapes:* Though blisters had seldom been a problem for me when hiking, they became one while on the Spanish portion of the Camino. It may have been the boots I wore, the trail surfaces, the heat, the hours day after day. Everyone's feet are different; anyone's feet can encounter new difficulties. Whatever the cause, I was not alone. People were glad to share their remedies.

  From a French woman, we learned of a two-inch wide, breathable cloth tape that I began to use extensively. I now wrap it around the balls of my feet and certain toes *before* problems arise. We also carry 3/4-inch wide breathable cloth tape, as well as *SpiroFlex*, for hot spots and *Compeed* for blisters. Buy the two-inch tape and *Compeed* in Spain. *2nd Skin* is another highly-regarded blister product and is available in the U.S. I highly recommend that you read John Vonhoff's *Fixing your Feet* to learn how to ward off foot problems.
- *Plastic basin:* lightweight, flexible, and folding—for soaking feet and washing clothes. In a pinch, you could use one or two freezer-weight, 2-gallon Ziplocs bags, if you can find them.
- *Water bottle:* one-liter, wide-mouth. Incidentally, a *wide-mouth* bottle works much better for mixing Tang, lemonade or dry milk powder, etc.). Ralph carried a 1.5 liter bottle. Almost all towns had a fountain with potable water so we did not need to carry water filters or purify-

ing tablets. (However, tablets weigh very little and could give peace-of-mind.)

Incidentally, a water bottle is useful for more than the obvious use as a beverage container. If you sleep cold, fill your bottle with hot water and put the bottle at the bottom of your sleeping bag, or against your body wherever you normally feel most chilled, and you will stay much warmer all night. (Be sure the top of your bottle is securely tightened.)

- *Swiss Army knife:* Ralph carries one with a couple of blades, a corkscrew, nail file, toothpick, tweezers, and several other tools. I carry a smaller version. At this time, such items can be carried on most airlines if in *checked* luggage.
- *Flashlight:* A mini-LED light is lightest, a Mini Maglite, with its two AA batteries weighs less than four ounces. A headlamp could be carried. Be sure that you can direct the light to your immediate area so that your roommates won't be kept awake while you read your dimestore novel.

Susan's Clothing

Most of your clothing should be of synthetic fibers because they dry quickly and "wick" perspiration away from your body so that you don't become chilled when you stop exercising.

For my shirts, pants, and skirt, I chose one basic color, navy blue, and built around it. You can choose any neutral color—such as black, navy blue, khaki, or tan. Use neck scarves to add flair if desired. (One of the women on the trail carried a *pareo,* a Tahitian-style length of fabric that can be wrapped around the waist and used as a skirt, around the body as a sarong, or over the shoulders as a shawl. She turned her pareo into a beautiful, feminine skirt that she enjoyed wearing when she wanted a change from her utilitarian hiking clothes.) Consider the following:

- *Skirt:* knit, length just above the knee. On our subsequent trip on Camino trails in France, I also carried a longer skirt because I noticed that the women in the rural areas dress more conservatively than those in the large cities.
- *Tee shirt:* short-sleeved knit, quick-dry synthetic.
- *Tee shirt:* cotton. Along the way, I bought a souvenir shirt for fun—which, being cotton, took forever to dry.
- *Blouse:* long-sleeved synthetic.
- *Pants:* 2 pairs (1 is optional), synthetic. Pair #1: Long with zip-off legs, Pair #2: Long with tapered legs. This pair is somewhat warmer, and more wind- and water-resistant.

UNDERWEAR
- *Slip, half:* black nylon.
- *Panties:* 3-pair, dark color.
- *Bra* or sportsbra.
- *Long underwear:* wicking, polypropylene or silk. I chose a synthetic black, long-sleeved top, which could also be used as outwear, and silk bottoms.

OUTERWEAR
- *Rain jacket:* waterproof, breathable, with "pit" (underarm) zips. The advantage of Goretex and similar fabrics is that they allow moisture (perspiration) to move through to the outside, but prevent it from coming inside.
- *Jackets:* down and fleece. I carry both—which may be overkill. (Down is light and warmer, but useless if wet. Fleece should be windproof and water-resistant.)
- *Rain pants:* waterproof, breathable preferred. Ankle zips preferable: it's much more convenient if you can put them on and take them off *without* removing your boots or shoes.
- *Pants:* fleece, black, nine-inch zipper at ankle for ease of getting on and off while wearing boots.
- *Hats:* a fleece cap (covering the ears) for cold days, and

a lightweight fabric hat for hot ones (mine, by Sunday Afternoons, has a large brim and also covers the back of my neck).

FOOTWEAR

- *Hiking boots:* above the ankle, or *running shoes* if you are used to hiking with them. (Use them with hiking poles.) Remember: your feet may swell a shoe size on long-distance hikes—buy accordingly.
- *Sandals:* blue, suede. In addition to hiking boots or shoes, an essential part of every pilgrim's gear is a pair of very light-weight, comfortable sandals for walking around to find food and to see the sights after the day's hike.
- *Socks:* Wrights, 3 pair. Many brands would work, but I like the fact that these are made of two layers: outer one of Merino wool, inner one of quick-drying synthetics. Three pairs gives you one on your feet, one for changing to, and one drying on a short line on your pack.

"LUXURIES" SUSAN CAN'T do without

- *Books:* Leisure reading. An expendable book that allows you to tear off pages as you go (or leave the book intact at a refugio for another traveler).
- *Notebook paper* and *pen* for journal writing.
- *Camera* and *film*: A compact APS Canon with zoom lens (prints). Ralph carries a Canon A95 digital camera.

On our flight to Spain, prior to 9/11, we were able to carry our backpacks, fully packed, on board, facilitating check-in at the airport and avoiding going to baggage claims at the end of the long flight. On our flight home, after 9/11, we were required to check our hiking poles and umbrellas. We'd have had to check our Swiss Army knives too, but because of our uncertainly about fluctuating regulations, we had given them away before we went to the airport.

THERE WAS NOTHING we lacked during our trip, but I did get awfully sick of wearing the same wardrobe day after day. I wanted to burn my tee shirts and pants when I got home, but I wasn't sure if synthetics would burn, so I just threw them out. Fifteen pounds is not a heavy load to carry, so a few extra clothing items do not make much difference. We were always reasonably clean and presentable. We washed clothes most nights, but if for some reason clothing did not dry by morning, we had extra. Skirts fall in the optional category, but they were a welcome change when we went to dinner.

Appendix

Who Are the Modern Day Pilgrims?

Of the nearly 94,000 making the pilgrimage in 2005, the vast majority were from Spain—52,928 compared to about 41,000 from all other countries combined. (The total for the Holy Year of 2004 was 180,000.) More than 92% of pilgrims were European, 4% from North America, and 2% from South America. By far the most travelers started in Sarria, followed by O Cebreiro, and then Roncesvalles. These numbers indicate the growing interest in making the pilgrimage to Santiago; when we hiked the Camino in 2001, 61,418 received the Compostela.

"Student" was the most named profession—18,827. Sailors outnumbered nuns—102 to 79 respectively. All ages travel the Camino; the largest number was for the 35–60 age group. In 2004, there were 59 people over the age of 80 who were awarded the prized *Compostela*.

More than 40% of the pilgrims in 2005 were women. Ninety-one percent declared their reason for making the pilgrimage was "religious" or "religious and other reasons."

Overwhelmingly, the greatest number traveled on foot (81%), with bicycle, horseback, and wheelchair carrying the others. Most went the French Way (the St. James Way); the fewest (of the categories given) went the English Way.

TOUR COMPANIES HAVE responded to Americans' increased awareness and interest in the Camino. Spain was already well-known for its cultural offerings, its regions of great scenic beauty, and its hospitality, but offering hiking trips so travelers could experience part of the Camino was something novel for the tour companies. When we consider the mushrooming growth of interest in adventure and exotic travel, and the rich experiences that the Camino offers, it's no wonder that once again many are making a pilgrimage.

Clearly, *any* visit to Spain offers the opportunity to enjoy the art, music, architecture, the food and wine, the people, but *walking* the Camino is a unique experience. Few will escape the sense of timelessness—identifying with those who have traveled the same path 100, or 500, or 1,000 years earlier.

The following statistics are from the Archidiocese of Compostela, www.archicompostela.org/statistics. Note that the official records record those who completed at least the last sixty-two miles (100 kilometers) on foot, 200 kilometers by bicycle, and registered at the Pilgrim Office to obtain the Cathedral's certificate of pilgrimage, the *Compostela*. It does not include those who did not apply for it, or who completed a segment of the trail and ended their trip elsewhere.

Occupations (top 8 categories)

Students	18,827
White-collar workers	16,552
Technicians	11,592
Freelancers (artists)	11.153
Pensioners (retired)	10,389
Teachers	7,886
Civil Servants	5,029
Workers	4,798

Method of travel

Foot	76,674
Bicycle	16,985
Horseback	242
Wheelchair	23

Countries of Origin (top 12)

Spain	52,928
Italy	7,430
Germany	7,155
France	5,909
Portugal	2,574
United States	2,047
Holland	1,610
United Kingdom	1,512
Austria	1,470
Canada	1,420
Belgium	1,283
Brazil	1,163

Month of Arrival

January	269
February	558
March	3,128
April	3,307
May	9,310
June	12,620
July	18,807
August	24,820
September	12,168
October	6,873
November	1,396
December	668

Routes (top 5)

French Way	79,396
Portuguese Way	5,508
Northern Way	3,984
Via de la Plata (Silver Way)	3,140
Primitive Way	1,028

Age Groups

0-12	962
13-18	8.896
19-35	32,666
35-60	40,897
More than 60	10,413

Modern-Day Juvenile Justice, Galician Style

In November of 2004, the following message came across the Go-Camino forum from Rosina Lila, an American woman who spends much of her year in Santiago researching the Camino:

"In what appears to be an innovative change in the old practice, six juvenile delinquents serving time in several Galicia prisons have been granted 'off time' to make the pilgrimage from Melide to Santiago. Further, a juvenile court judge will accompany them as well as some educators and social therapists.

"The youngsters, convicted of committing 'crimes of violence' will have to return to their prisons to complete their sentence (apparently there is no indeterminate sentencing in Spain); the pilgrimage will afford them an opportunity to spend some time in the open air, with the hope that it will also further their social rehabilitation.

"This is somewhat different from the OIKOTEN, juvenile offenders that Belgium sends on the pilgrimage sometimes in lieu of jail time. While some first-time criminal offenders in Spain have also been given such options, they have been convicted of nonviolent crimes, such as possession of drugs, etc. The six now on the Camino are the first ones to just be given 'time off' to make the pilgrimage."

Belgium's Oikoten community attempts to provide youngsters alternatives to "criminal or otherwise unacceptable behavior." Since the program began in 1982, more than 160 young men and women have been accompanied on a walk to Santiago de Compostela.

Walter Lombaert, who lives and works at the Oikoten Community, accompanied two juvenile boys on a four-month hike from Belgium to Compostela. He later reported that the participants returned home changed: with a greater sense of self-respect and a new direction for their lives. (Oikoten was originally inspired by VisionQuest, a U.S. program that takes at-risk juveniles on survival trips.)

Inside the church at Frómista

Bibliography

Andrew, David. "Salud!" *Costco Connection: A Lifestyle Magazine for Small Business.* Issaquah, WA: Feb., 2003, 36.

Aviva, Elyn. *Following the Milky Way: A pilgrimage on the Camino de Santiago,* Second ed. Boulder, CO: Pilgrims' Progress, Inc., 2001.

Bisset, William, editor. *1. The Camino Francés: Saint-Jean-Pied-de-Port to Santiago de Compostela. Pilgrim Guides to Spain.* London, England: Confraternity of Saint James, 2005.

Brierley, John. *A Pilgrim's Guide to the Camino de Santiago: Camino Francés:* Scotland: Camino Guides, 2006.

Coelho, Paulo, *The Pilgrimage.* New York: Harper Perennial/Harper Collins, 1992.

Davies, Bethan & Cole, Ben. *Walking the Camino de Santiago: From St. Jean-Pied-de-Port to Santiago de Compostela and on to Finisterre.* Vancouver, BC: Pili Pala Press, 2003.

Frey, Nancy. *Pilgrim Stories: On and Off the Road to Santiago.* Univ. of California Press, Berkeley, CA., 1998.

Gitlitz, David M. and Davidson, Linda Kay. *The Pilgrimage Road to Santiago: The Complete Cultural Handbook.* New York, NY: St. Martin's Griffin, 2000.

Hall, James. English translation of Hoinacki, Lee. *El Camino: Walking to Santiago de Compostela.* Penn State Press, University Park, PN, 1996.

Hitt, Jack. Off the Road: A Modern-Day Walk Down the Pilgrim's Route into Spain. New York, NY: Simon &

Schuster, 2005.

Jardine, Ray. *Beyond Backpacking. Ray Jardine's Guide to Lightweight Hiking.* LaPine, OR, 2000.

Keller, Shelly, "Seasonings." *Solano Magazine.* Fairfield, CA: Premiere issue, Dec. 2003, 98.

Kenney, Sue. *My Camino.* Toronto, Canada: White Knight Publications, 2004.

Kenney, Sue. *Stone by Stone,* a CD. A narration of a woman's experiences of the Camino.

Laffi, Domenico. *A Journey to the West: The Diary of a Seventeenth-Century Pilgrim from Bologna to Santiago De Compostela.* Trans. James Hall. Leiden: Primavera Press, 1997.

Michener, James A. *Iberia.* New York: Random House, Inc., 1968).

Nooteboom, Gees. *Roads to Santiago: A Modern Day Pilgrimage through Spain.* Orlando, FL: Harcourt, Inc., 1992.

Norton, Andre. Various. Chapter 1 quotation used with permission. www.andrenorton.com

The Pilgrim's Guide to Santiago de Compostela. Codex Calixtinus, Book Five, Chapter VI. Trans. William Melczer. New York: Italica Press, 1993, 89.

Roddis, Miles, Nancy Frey & Jose Placer, Matthew Fletcher, John Noble. *Walking in Spain.* Victoria, Australia: Lonely Planet Publications Ply., 2003.

Spicer, Dorothy Gladys, *Festivals of Western Europe.* New York: H.W. Wilson Company, 1958.

Steves, Rick. *Paris 2004.* Emeryville, CA: Avalon Travel Publishing, 2004.

Vonhoff, John. *Fixing your Feet: Prevention and Treatments for Athletes:* third ed., Berkeley, CA: Wilderness Press, June, 2004.

www.sanfermin.com. Everything you need to know about Pamplona and the annual running of the bulls.

List of Photographs

Index

About the Author

Susan Alcorn has always enjoyed hiking. She began back-packing in 1989, shortly after she and her husband, Ralph, were married. Her backpacking adventures led her to write and publish *We're in the Mountains Not Over the Hill—Tales and Tips from Seasoned Women Backpackers,* which encourages and supports men and women of *all* ages to find the challenges and rewards of the trail.

After their walk on Spain's *Camino de Santiago,* Susan and Ralph decided to explore one of the four major routes in France that connects with the Spanish trail. In May 2004, they began their hike following the Chemin St. Jacques (via GR 65) starting in the small town of Le Puy-en-Velay. They walked to Figeac (150 miles/242 km.). In September 2005, they returned to Figeac to continue westward and reached Aire-Sur-l'Adour (200 miles/323 km.). In 2006, they hope to return to France to complete the final portion of the Le Puy route to Roncesvalles, and then continue on into Spain to hike the 100 miles from León to Ponferrada they had to bypass in 2001.

Susan has retired from teaching elementary school. She and Ralph live in the San Francisco Bay Area, where they happily take advantage of the area's excellent regional parks and trails. The couple presently enjoy not only their travels (with subsequent writing and publishing), but also being at home to enjoy friends, family, and Zydeco music.

Ordering this or other books by Susan Alcorn

IF YOU ENJOYED *Camino Chronicle: Walking to Santiago* and would like to order additional copies for yourself or friends, please check with your local bookstore, favorite online bookseller or visit www.backpack45.com and place your order directly with the publisher.

WE'RE IN THE *Mountains Not Over the Hill: Tales and Tips from Seasoned Women Backpackers.* $14.95. ISBN #0-936034-02-5.

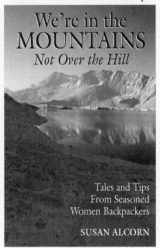

Awarded "Best Travel/Adventure Book 2005." Bay Area Independent Publishers Association (BAIPA).

THREE DOZEN WOMEN, in the prime of their lives, take you backpacking in the Sierra, the Rockies, the Appalachians and more. This compelling collage of stories and advice combines honesty, insight and humor with practical wisdom and proven tips to inspire women and men of all ages.

We're in the Mountains Not Over the Hill "debunks the myth that only the young and fearless and male can enjoy backcountry travel..." "[the book] takes the mystique out of the sport of backpacking and makes it understandable and accessible to any woman, anywhere, of any age." Amy Racina, author of *Angels in the Wilderness.*